W9-BNG-816

THE PLAYGROUND AS
MUSIC TEACHER

THE
PLAYGROUND AS
MUSIC TEACHER

An Introduction to
Music Through Games

MADELEINE CARABO-CONE

HARPER & BROTHERS, PUBLISHERS, NEW YORK

TABLE OF CONTENTS

2. INTERMEDIATE GAMES

3. ADVANCED GAMES

APPENDIX

FOREWORD

By Richard S. Crutchfield, Professor of Psychology and Associate Director, Institute of Personality Assessment and Research, University of California, Berkeley

Since young children regularly demonstrate an astonishing capability for mastery of complex language, there is no good reason to suppose that they are any less capable of assimilating the elementary language of music—its symbols and notations. In this book Madeleine Carabo-Cone has created highly ingenious methods for teaching the child such elements of music. In an unobtrusive but thoroughly effective way the methods make use of sound psychological principles of learning by the child.

Recent findings and theories by psychologists are placing ever greater stress on the critical role in the learning process played by kinesthetic "feedback" produced by body movements. The methods described in this book rely heavily on this important function, exploiting skillfully the natural primacy of body movements in the child's play activities.

The methods also make the most of psychological principles concerning the crucial significance of self-involvements by the child in the learning process. The pervasive readiness of the child to respond to dynamic, expressive, and affective qualities of the perceptual objects in his world is cleverly utilized in these methods, serving to make the musical symbols "come alive."

And by directed play with giant-scale representations of the musical staff and other symbols, the child literally "gets into" and "acts inside" the musical framework.

Speaking from the point of view of a psychologist, I find the book sensible and stimulating; speaking as a parent, my only criticism of the book is that it comes out too late for my own children's musical education.

PREFACE

As a nation we will not tolerate illiteracy. Yet although we profess to have ambition for a superior musical culture, we are complacent about large masses of our people who can sing only the songs they hear and know only the music that is played for them. If we are in earnest about developing a musical culture as fine as any in the world, then we must realize that such a culture can thrive best in an atmosphere of musical literacy.

There are many people who feel that music study is an isolated specialty whose omission can have no noticeable effect on the rest of the curriculum. Few realize that the sharpened sensory perceptions acquired through recognition of differences in pitch and tone quality, the development of rhythmic coordinations, the visual alertness acquired in rapid reactions to the space relationships of the music staff carry over into a livelier response to the tone-colors and rhythmics of prose, poetry, painting, and other arts, while the intensive concentration developed is an invaluable aid in the study of all academic subjects.

The January 1958 issue of the *Music Educators Journal* contained a review of the pamphlet, *"Playground Music: The Playground Gets a Musical Playing Field."* The reviewer wrote:

The playground can help the child hop-skip his way to familiarity with musical notation. That's what Madeleine Carabo-Cone thinks and she explains and proves it by the use of a musical playing field. It's simple. . . .

If children can aquire a foundation for musical literacy with a mere hop, skip, and jump, what excuse can there be for denying them this knowledge?

There remains one more question: "Why not wait until they are older?"

If we wait until the early adolescent years to develop music-reading skills, we find that young people today, even at the ages of twelve and thirteen, are so beset with the serious problem of college preparation and the heavy schedule of athletic and other extracurricular events, not to mention the sociological phenomenon of "going steady," that even though they often express a desire to learn to play a musical instrument at this time, they have neither the time nor patience. Before any fluency at an instrument is possible, the fundamentals of reading and rhythm must be ingrained.

Early childhood is plainly the best time to absorb these fundamentals easily.

For some years, our entire musical education for the young child has been based on the premise that it is harmful to introduce a child to the intricate symbols of music notation too early. Professors in music education and many specialists in the field of early childhood education have felt that looking at music symbols is too great a visual strain for the young child, and that his experience should be confined to spontaneous body movement in response to sound.

We are now beginning to realize that reading music is one of the great stumbling blocks for most students. Even the five-lined, single staff songbook used in school does not prepare the child for the Grand Staff (or bass and treble staff combined) that is used for piano music. Nor does the child come to the study of music, as to reading, having absorbed from his environment familiarity with some of the symbols.

Incredible as it now seems, several years ago there was so much prejudice among educators against exposing young children to visual symbols that for almost a ten-year period the letters of the alphabet were banished from the decoration of nursery furniture and toys. However, children still noticed and absorbed brand names and street signs. What child reaches the first grade without being able to recognize a STOP sign or a Coca Cola bottle?

Therefore, despite every precaution, children acquire a certain familiarity with words that makes their formal study of reading a *natural progression*.

The author noticed that with her own children the effect of this early exposure was to awaken an interest in learning to read. The same principle can be applied to music learning.

Children of all ages can enjoy a variation in their favorite games, and at the same time absorb unconsciously and effortlessly the entire framework for the reading of music. On the musical playing field there will be no strain of delicate eye muscles, only the large muscles of legs and arms in happy motion.

ACKNOWLEDGMENTS

The author acknowledges her indebtedness to her husband and colleague, Harold Cone, for his assistance with the musical examples in particular and his cooperation throughout her entire project in general. Without his sympathetic support this book could not have been written.

The author also acknowledges with gratitude the assistance of Sushma Rani Mathur of New Delhi, India, and May Tse-Ching Tsao of Hong Kong, who during the summer of 1958 worked in close collaboration with her to produce the finished drawings from her rough sketches and suggestions.

She appreciates the interest and patience shown by Mr. H. G. Finney, of Oscar Schmidt-International Inc., Jersey City, New Jersey, manufacturers of the Autoharp, in permitting her to experiment with his company's product in an effort to convert it into an audio-visual-tactile supplement to the playground music staff.

To Letitia Pendleton Thomas, Richard McAdoo, and Ordway Tead go her heartfelt thanks for editorial guidance along the thorny path of book production.

INTRODUCTION

To be deeply rooted, learning must be integrated from the beginning. This is especially true of any skill that involves intricate physical coordination.

For this reason, the author feels that the playing of games on a musical playing field, besides furnishing variety in recreation, contributes much to laying a sound foundation for the study of music.

Psychologists agree that acting is a child's substitute for abstract thinking. Motor behavior is the most conspicuous characteristic in childhood. The games described in this book are designed to channel the child's motor energy into learning activities.

Piaget and others who specialize in the psychology of early childhood have shown that the child invests the objects around him with life and constructs for himself a private magical world. Encouraged to identify himself with the material to be learned, the child absorbs the meaning of music symbols in the process of dramatizing them. The magic Middle C line mentioned in so many of the games, appeals to the child's own brand of fantasy and still serves as a realistic and valid explanation of one of the most important points on the musical staff.

By constantly comparing the space relationships of the staff to himself and the time-values of notes to his own movements, he is using his innate learning processes to acquire concepts through an immediate and personal experience.

According to psychological tests the attention span of the young child is limited, yet in these games, because of the physical relief of the muscular activity, it is never forced beyond his level of endurance or understanding. Through play and dramatic interpretation his attention span is actually lengthened.

If he is capable of only a few impressions these are reinforced by all of his senses and motor powers acting together until a concept slowly develops. In each game he combines, relates, matches, compares the staff, the notes, and the rhythms to his own activities.

Many repetitions which are subtly disguised as new games give him the unconscious incidental learning that allows him to make a natural and happy progress. Because every child needs many opportunities to succeed, particularly in music where there have been so many lost by the wayside because of feelings of failure, each game becomes a victory over a subject matter that has heretofore been considered too difficult for children. Every time a child reads a note himself and finds it on the keyboard, he is so bolstered up by his own success that he is carried swiftly along the road to learning.

The physical setup for the playing of the musical games, combined with creative and dramatic elements, introduces the basic requirements for learning music.

Associated sounds, physical movement, tactile experience, space relationships through personal comparison—all provide a "learning-in-depth." Even at an elementary level, these games develop instantaneous coordinations, keener perceptions and visual focus, and they demand constant memory discipline, all of which are literally "brought into play."

The idea of painting ten lines on a playground may appear to be a burdensome task for many people. However, when we think of the vast amounts of money and energy wasted in trying to teach music to unwilling youngsters, does it not seem a comparatively simple expedient to provide on our playgrounds and schoolyards a game court that will give every child the framework for reading music whenever he has the desire and opportunity?

The Playground as Music Teacher offers to playground directors, community centers, schools, and camps, a program of classic childhood games translated into music-learning activities on a music-staff playing field. Many of these are traditional "street" games that pass mysteriously from generation to generation and are as natural to a child's life as growing taller or getting new teeth.

Although these games have been adapted to the musical playing field for music-learning purposes, they retain their intrinsic elements of suspense, excitement, cunning, competition, secrecy, energy-release, muscular activity, and sheer luck.

For the fullest kind of elementary music program they should be supplemented by songbooks, records, instruments, and other music materials. By itself, this book is an outdoor-indoor educational recreation program that can be directed successfully by anyone who enjoys working with children. It is addressed particularly to all those (recreation leaders, elementary classroom teachers, Scout and community group leaders, summer and day camp personnel, etc.) who in dealing with children feel a strong obligation to spread before their charges the greatest possible cultural opportunities.

For the benefit of those who have had no musical training whatsoever, two special chapters have been provided. These contain the specific musical knowledge underlying the games.

The material in Chapter 1 equips the reader to lead all the elementary games. This section pertains to familiarity with the music staff itself and to a general music-reading readiness, as well as to the basic elements of rhythm, time-values, and coordination. The material in Chapter 2 starts an acquaintance with the keyboard and lays the musical groundwork for the intermediate and advanced games.

One could paraphrase the slogan of certain training schools—"learn while you earn" to "Learn some music while you play games with children." After refereeing on the music-staff playing field and settling the differences between Half Note and Whole Note, the leader will have had sufficient active participation to tackle Chapter 2.

The elementary games are primarily for children from five to seven. The intermediate games are for those seven and eight-year-olds who have mastered the elementary games. The advanced games are for children from seven to ten after they have had a wide sampling of both elementary and intermediate games.

To be used in conjunction with all these games for every age group are the time-value, rhythm, and coordination games. Certain activities and games such as Banners Flying (Parade of the Time-Value Regiments), Feeling the Beat, Conducting Designs, Counting Measures, Counting on the Fingers, Measure Rulers, Story Telling, and Time-Value Hand Movements are so fundamental that they never outgrow their usefulness.

A special feature of this book is the coincidence of an alphabetical and a progressive arrangement of games within each section.

Each game in each classification has its learning goal clearly defined. The program as a whole aims to offer musical literacy to all children instead of to a random few.

This book is not an attempt to undermine the music teacher's role but rather to lend him needed support by making his work doubly effective. The specialist has greater limitation on his time. Coming in contact with a group of children who have already been exposed to musical concepts and musical language, he can go "full steam ahead" in giving the best of his highly specialized training. The groundwork for rewarding musical experience in later years can be laid by those who are able to be with children for longer periods of time in a practical and patient guidance of their play activities.

Since both educators and parents are currently aware of the need for intellectual stimulus to equip our children to meet the problems of the world of tomorrow, the author looks forward to profound changes in educational programs for the young child. She feels there will be less reluctance to expose children to an early acquaintance with any project that will lead to a greater mastery of a highly technical subject. When even a technical subject can be presented through the natural expression of play, not only need there be no fear of maladjustment, but the method could be adapted to a wide range of subjects. At the same time, this approach serves to offset the lure of a comic-book culture and to attract the young toward the challenging world of the mind where achievement is the prize.

I

Orientation and Preparation

1. BACKGROUND FOR ELEMENTARY GAMES

This chapter is specially planned to enable recreation leaders or teachers without previous musical training to organize and direct the elementary games in this book. Therefore, the information is confined to that which is necessary for the understanding and supervision of these games. It is recommended that prospective leaders work out the demonstrations and projects in advance of meetings with their groups.

Since the material contained in Chapter 2 concerns certain games in the intermediate and advanced categories, it is not necessary that it be studied until Chapter 1 has been thoroughly mastered and put into practice.

Because all of the information in this chapter must ultimately be transmitted to the children, it contains special activities and demonstrations specifically planned for children. Particular projects, such as making a model keyboard, various staff charts, etc., serve to establish a bare outline which will be filled in during the course of the ensuing games and activities.

THE MUSICAL PLAYING FIELD

The musical playing field represents the Grand Staff of music, which consists of eleven lines, the center one existing only in the imagination. (Figs. 22, 34) The center line, or what would be the sixth line from the bottom if it were visible, is called the Magic Line of Middle C. (Naturally, anything magical appeals to children.) A little of this Magic Line will suddenly appear as a small black line going through the center of any note placed on it. Such notes are called Middle C, also, since every line and every space on the music staff playing field has an alphabetical name which it gives to any note placed on it.

PLACEMENT OF THE NOTES

The notes in these games will be cutout paper symbols or they will be personified by the children themselves, in most cases wearing the paper symbols over their arms or heads.

All the notes used in these games except the whole note consist of a round head and an attached stick or line. A circle and a stick are two of the simplest forms that very young children can identify.

Whenever a note, either a cutout note or a child acting as a note is to be placed on a line and therefore to take the name of that line, the line must go through the center of the cutout notes, or under the center of the soles of the feet in the case of a "note-child."

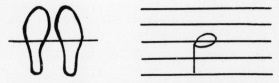

FIG. 1.   Soles of feet on line; note on line.

If a note is to occupy a space and therefore to take the name of that space, neither the cutout note nor the soles of the feet may extend beyond the lines on either side of the space, but must be entirely contained within that space. Therefore cutout

4

notes must be carefully measured to fit between the lines of the musical playing field.

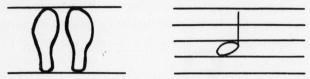

FIG. 2.   Soles of feet within space; note in space.

THE STAFF AND ITS MUSICAL ALPHABET

The musical alphabet extends from A to G, seven different letters in all. After every G, it begins again with A.

The bottom line is G. Therefore the space directly above the bottom line is A, the second line B, the second space (or space above the second line) is C, etc. (See Fig. 22.)

Throughout the games, this going up the staff while going forward in the alphabet will be dramatized by facing forward as the children walk up the music-staff playing field and simultaneously recite the musical alphabet.

As they walk downward from the top line of the Grand Staff (F) they will step backward, saying the alphabet in reverse.

THE BASS CLEF (F Clef) AND THE
BASS CLEF STAFF

Numbering the lines from the bottom, the first five lines from the bottom comprise the bass clef staff, and the symbol that begins twisting around the fourth line from the bottom at the extreme left, looking like a monkey's tail wound around a bar, is called the F clef or bass clef.

A five-year old Swiss child newly arrived in America told her mother that Mrs. Cone had said that the fourth line was a monkey. Her mother asked me about this and I denied ever

5

having referred to a monkey. The mystery was solved when the mother realized that the German word for monkey was *äfflein*. I was talking about the "F line." But after that incident, the F clef began to look like a monkey's tail to me, too.

FIG. 3.   Bass clef.

The F clef or bass clef has two dots that go on either side of the fourth line which is called F. To prove this for yourself, start at the bottom line which is G. The space above is A, the second line is B, the space above the second line is C, the third line is D, the space above the third line is E, and when you arrive at the fourth line, that line is F.

The two dots that surround and guard the F line make a vivid landmark. They are the vestiges of a Gothic letter F that was used to mark the F line.

FIG. 4.   An early F clef.

In these games, we will refer to the bass clef very often as the F clef because it marks the place where F is.

6

Remember that the fourth line from the bottom, the F line, lies between the two dots of the F clef. The F clef is the other name of the bass clef.

These names will be used interchangeably. It is helpful to begin with the name F clef because it serves not only as a name but actually identifies the line that goes through its starting point and in between its two dots.

The five bottom lines of the music-staff playing field or Grand Staff comprise the territory belonging to this F or bass clef. We refer to these five lines as the bass clef staff or F clef staff. When we correlate the staff to the piano, we will find that these lines and spaces of the bass staff represent low sounds.

THE MAGIC LINE

Above the bottom five lines lies a special territory. On music paper it is completely white, but across the middle of this section stretches the imaginary Middle C line, which we have termed the Magic Line, described on p. 4. Once you recognize that there is a line there, you immediately have a space on either side of the Magic Line.

As you remember, the fourth line from the bottom of the bass staff was F, the space above it is G and after a G the alphabet is repeated. Therefore the top line, the fifth line of the bass staff, is A. The space above this top bass line is B. Then comes the magic Middle C line and the space above that is D. Children like to think of the White Territory in the center of the playing field as "B-C-D Land."

A note placed on Middle C will make a part of that Magic Line turn black, but only enough of it to go through the center of the round head of the note. WARNING: There are other notes above and below the whole Grand Staff in musical literature that look like this note but in order to be Middle C the note

7

must appear on a tiny line of its own between the bottom five lines (bass staff) and the top five lines (treble or G staff).

Beginning piano students often mistake any note that has a small line through it for Middle C. There are other imaginary lines above and below the whole Grand Staff that act the same way. When a note is placed on them, the line comes through the note and shows its true color—black. In these games, the

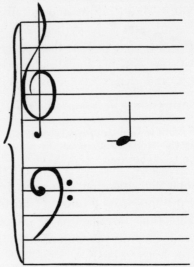

FIG. 5.   Middle C.

imaginary lines above and below the staff which are called "leger lines" will be only touched upon.

If we succeed in ingraining the image of the Grand Staff itself, we will have a firm foundation for all further musical knowledge.

When there is no note on B, Middle C, or D in the center section of the Grand Staff, the territory will remain white. If a note is to appear on Middle C, it will have its own private line running through its center, showing a tiny bit at each side of the note itself.

8

A note may appear on the space below Middle C or on the space above it without requiring that the Middle C line show at all. The Middle C remains unseen for a note on space B below it or space D above it, except when its appearance is

Fig. 6. Arrows show lines from which notes have been "borrowed." When the bass staff needs to show notes higher than Middle C, it borrows from lines in the treble staff. When the treble staff needs to show notes lower than Middle C, it borrows from the bass staff.

needed for the sake of clarity as in chords, where B and D occur in combinations with other tones, all of which must be sounded simultaneously, or as in an expansion of the range of either staff.*

TREBLE OR G CLEF STAFF

Above this white section is the G clef or treble clef staff of five lines and the spaces created by these five lines. Commonly called the treble clef, it is also the G clef because it marks the line G. Like the Gothic letter F that was used to mark the line F, a Gothic letter G was used to mark the G line.

In olden times, sometimes only a circular sign was used—a special Gothic letter G—and the second of the five lines had to

* Such exceptions need not concern the reader of this book for only B, C, and D appear in the White Territory in the course of the games described.

9

go through this circle, thus being indentified as the line G. Today, the second line of the five treble lines must still go through the circular part of the G clef as we have it now.

FIG. 7.   Early G clefs.

Knowing that the second line is G, it is simple to figure out the names of all the other lines and spaces. The space below G must be F and the line below that which is the bottom or first line of the treble staff is E. The space above the G line must be A and so on up the rest of the treble staff.

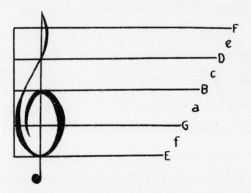

FIG. 8.   Alphabetical names of lines and spaces in the treble staff.

This approach associates the alphabetical name with its location on the staff and is much more meaningful than memorizing "Every Good Boy Does Fine" (the first letter of each word being the name of a line in the treble clef) and memorizing the letters in the world "F-A-C-E-" as the names of the spaces in the treble staff. Not only is there no relationship suggested from line to space to line in these artificial memory helps, as there is in the alphabetical progression of line E to space F to line G, for example, but the bass clef is entirely neglected.

This relationship is of the utmost importance and the ability to go up the staff thinking the alphabet forward and also to come down the staff thinking the alphabet backward is a large part of the problem of reading music.

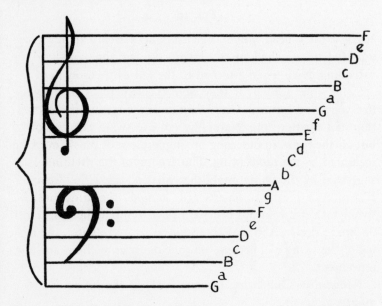

FIG. 9. The Grand Staff—alphabetical names of lines and spaces.

Most of the songbooks that children use in school show only the treble or G clef staff of five lines so here again there is no helpful "carry-over" to the piano music with which they are confronted when they begin to take lessons.

Only the Grand Staff which forms our playing field can pro-vide a complete framework for music reading on any instrument.

11

THE NOTES AND THEIR TIME-VALUES

Quarter Note

A quarter note looks like this:

FIG. 10.

It has a thick head, solidly filled in, and a stem extending upward when attached on the right side of the note-head or extending down when attached to the left of the note-head.*

Swing your arms as if they were the two ropes of a swing, backward and forward. One swing in one direction is the duration of a quarter note. Naturally, you can swing fast or slowly, but all the notes in one song or simple piece of music must be measured by the *same* swing. This feeling of the rhythmic beat suggested by the swing establishes what is called the "tempo." If a piece is meant to have a fast "tempo" the arms must be swung fast; if it is meant to have a slow "tempo" the arms must be swung slowly. Above all, keep the swing *even*. Later, the feeling of the swing will become subconcious even without any arm movement.

Remember: One swing (or one beat) is the time-value of a quarter note.

Half Note

A half note has a "hole in its head" and it also has a stem. Allow two swings of the arms, first backward then forward, for the time-value or duration of a half note. Sing or say, "Ha–lf"

---

* The child can imitate this stem placement on any given note by stretching his right arm straight up toward the sky or his left arm straight down toward the ground, as the case may be. All stemmed notes use this "up-on-the-right" or "down-on-the-left" placement.

while you swing both arms together, first backward then forward. If you sing, "Ha-alf," thinking two syllables but singing one unbroken tone every time both arms together swing backward then forward (two swings), you will be singing in half notes.

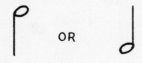

OR

FIG. 11.

A Dotted Half Note

A dotted half note looks just like a half note except that it is followed by a dot. The dot represents the addition of half the time-value of the note to which it is attached. A half note is worth two swings. Since half of two is one, the dot represents this one swing to be added. The half note followed by a dot gets three swings or beats (two plus half of that two).

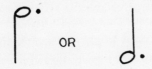

OR

FIG. 12.

If the dot followed a note of a different time-value it would still be worth exactly half of the time-value of the note it followed. Since a whole note is worth four swings, a whole note followed by a dot would be worth the four of the whole note plus half of that four—altogether six swings. If one half note were equal to an hour, a dotted half note would equal an hour and a half.

This series of games will deal only with the dotted half notes.

Whole Note

The whole note gets four swings. It has a "hole in its head" but *no* stem and resembles a doughnut, a tire, or a Lifesaver

13

candy. A quarter note is a quarter or one-fourth of a whole note.

FIG. 13.

Eighth Notes

Two eighth notes together are worth as much as one quarter note or one swing. Imagine saying a word of two syllables such as "swinging," to one swing of the arms in either direction. Each

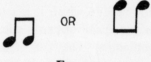

OR

FIG. 14.

syllable denotes one of these eighth notes; the pair signifies the whole word and gets a single swing. (A single swing is represented by both arms swinging in one direction, either backward or forward.)

Notice that the eighths have filled-in heads just like the quarter notes. They have stems just like the quarter notes. A single eighth note looks like a quarter note with a little flag on the end of the stick.

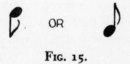

OR

FIG. 15.

The bar connecting the two stems of a pair of eighths is a convenient device for indicating a flag apiece. In each case the flag—

14

or its equivalent section on the bar—indicates a quarter note cut in half.*

We will not go beyond eighth notes in these play activities.

SYLLABLES AND SWINGS

Think of each note as a syllable. Let a quarter note sound as if you sang, "Lah!" Swing your arms backward and sing, "Lah" at the same time.

For a half note swing your arms first backward and then forward as you sing, "Lah-ah," but let the two syllables melt into each other without a break. Just think two syllables but sing them without a break. The two swings will make you feel two beats.

For a dotted half note, swing your arms back, forward, back, simultaneously thinking three separate syllables, "Lah-ah-ah" but singing them without a break. The half note is "Lah-ah" and the dot is an additional "ah."

For a whole note, swing backward, forward, backward, forward—four swings—simultaneously thinking four syllables,

---

* The quarter is one fourth of a whole note. This is important to bear in mind when considering the mathematics of these time divisions. A half note is two swings or one half of a whole note (four swings). Since a quarter note may be represented by the fraction 1/4, that fraction (1/4) divided in half is 1/8.

One flag on an eighth note shows that the note is one half of a quarter note. Add another flag to an eighth note and you have cut an eighth note in half. You now have half of an eighth note or a sixteenth note.

1/8 equals 1/2 of 1/4

1/16 equals 1/2 of 1/8

FIG. 16.

The flag says, "Cut what you have in half!"

15

"Lah-ah-ah-ah," but singing them in one continuous, unbroken tone.

For a pair of eighth notes, swing the arms backward and sing, "Lah-lah," *two* syllables to the *one* swing.

ACQUAINTANCE WITH THE KEYBOARD

Black Key Fingers

Have you noticed how often the picture of a pointed finger is used as a guide, showing the way to some special place? On the piano keyboard, there are black key "fingers" that point the way to special places too. Instead of using one pointed finger as a guide, the keyboard uses a pair of them (the Black Key Twins) and also a group of three black key fingers (the Black Key Triplets). The twin fingers will tell us where C, D, and E are, and the triplet fingers will point out F, G, A, and B. Since there are no other alphabet names to know, we have all the information we need.

Black Key Twins (Our Two-Finger Mitts)

If you have an old black glove whose mate you have lost, perhaps you won't mind cutting off the fingers. Put glove fingers on the index and middle fingers of your left hand. These will be your twin finger mitts for demonstrations to children.

Find a pair of black keys on the piano and gently press them down with your black key mitts so gently that no sound is made. Once down, keep them down. Bend the thumb of the right hand under so you can concentrate on the index, middle, and ring fingers of your right hand. With these right hand white key fingers, play the three neighboring white keys that surround your Black Key Twins. Press down the white keys at the back edge of the keyboard directly in front of the wooden panel. The purpose of this is to avoid being distracted by the different shapes of the keys.

16

The first white key to the left of the Black Key Twins is C. The next white key which lies between the two black key fingers is D and the white key to the right of the two black fingers is E. (Play the C with right hand index finger, D with the right middle finger, and E with the right ring finger.)

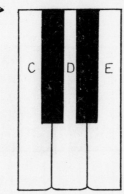

FIG. 17. Three white keys and Black Key Twins.

By following the same procedure with every pair of black keys on the whole keyboard, you will find that there are seven of them, and each pair is surrounded by the three white keys, C, D, and E.

After finding all the C, D, and E white keys as one group, go through the keyboard again and find all the C's by themselves, all the D's, and all the E's. The C to the left of the *center* pair of black keys is Middle C.

Black Key Triplets

Add one more of those black glove fingers to your left hand so that your three fingers (index, middle, and ring) of the left hand will now be wearing their black key costumes.

Place these fingers lightly on a group of three black piano keys, pressing them down so that they make no sound. We want

17

to hear only the four white keys surrounding them. Again bend the right thumb back slightly and use the remaining four fingers to play the four white keys that surround the Black Key Triplets. Again press the keys down at the back of the keyboard, near the wooden panel.

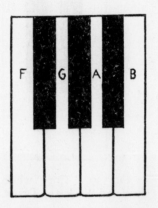

Fig. 18. Four white keys and Black Key Triplets.

The first white key to the left of our triplet black keys is F, which is followed by G and A, with B as the white key to the right of the three black fingers.

Find all the groups of three black keys and name the four white keys around them, F, G, A, and B. See how many complete groups like these there are in the entire keyboard. Find all the F's separately, all the G's, all the A's, and all the B's.

The second G up from the left of the keyboard is the G on the bottom line of the bass staff; the third F up from the left of the keyboard is the F line that lies between the two dots of the F clef; and the fourth G (again counting from the left) is the G line that goes through the lower part of the G clef.

18

MAKING A MODEL KEYBOARD

Hold a piece of tracing paper over the center section of the keyboard from C to B, which contains the three white keys C, D, and E around the twin black key "fingers" and also the four white keys F, G, A, and B surrounding the three black key "fingers."

Hold the paper above the twin black keys with the fingers of your left hand. Then draw lightly with pencil the ouside outline of the white key C (which is to the left of the two black "fingers"). Bring your pencil to the front of the keyboard across the white key C to the right, and outline six more white keys through B, which lies at the right of the three black "fingers." Now outline the white key B, finishing at the wooden panel behind the keyboard.

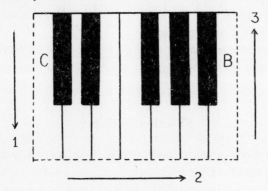

Fig. 19. Keyboard cutout.

Now outline the edges of the black keys, and indicate the separations between the white keys. Then you are ready to remove the paper to a table, and correct the lines with a ruler so that they are all straight and darker before you transfer the design to sturdier paper. It will then be easier to handle.

Each child should make seven of these units since seven comprise the whole keyboard (with the exception of one extra white key at the top right which is another C that would begin an additional unit). There are also two white keys and one black key left over at the bottom or extreme left of the keyboard.

Bear in mind that there are only seven complete units made up of the seven white keys from C to the next B above, together with the five black keys (the twins and the triplets) within this group.

The children should fill in the black keys until they look solid black, and tape the seven units together, so that, spread out, they make a model keyboard.

MERGING KEYBOARD AND STAFF

Since every line and space on our musical playing field has its corresponding white key on the piano, we must mentally transfer to the piano the Grand Staff of eleven lines (center one imaginary) and ten spaces.

The first step in relating the lines of the musical playing field to the white keys on the piano is to make the following staff charts.

STAFF CHART I

Take a piece of posterboard, white or yellow, six inches high (five and a half inches for spinets) and twenty-one inches wide, a pencil, a pale crayon, a felt nib marking pen, and a supply of masking tape.

Place the paper so that the twenty-one inch width is behind the back edge of the piano keys. It should stand up, resting against the wooden panel that extends in back of the keyboard. The center of the paper should be brought to the center of the Middle C of the piano. (As you remember, Middle C is the white key to the left of the center pair of black keys.) Make a pencil mark in the center of your paper to indicate the center of the Middle C piano key. To the left of this mark, make five more points about one and seven-eighths of an inch apart. Check carefully with your keyboard, so that each pencil mark coincides with the center of every *other* key to the left of the Middle C mark. Do the same to the right of Middle C. Each pencil mark should now coincide with the center of each corresponding piano key, which is every *other* key both to the left and to the right of Middle C.

Remove the paper to a table and draw vertical lines from the top of the paper two-thirds of the way down. Follow the pencil marks for the spacing of the lines. Make *no* line for Middle C. From the end of the lines continuing to the bottom edge of the paper, make a vertical row of the alphabet names of the lines in capital letters, omitting Middle C.

Putting in the Clefs

Turn your paper so that the lines are horizontal and the lettering is at the extreme right. The bottom five lines are the five lines of the F clef or bass clef staff. At the left, put in the F clef on the fourth line F. Add two heavy dots to the right of this clef, one above and one below the fourth line. Your bass clef and staff are now complete.

The five lines above the Middle C point represent the treble clef. Draw the G clef, by starting below the first of these five treble lines. Make a straight vertical line that extends a short distance above the top staff line. Make a right curve with your pencil as illustrated, bringing your line back to cross the fourth staff line to the left of the vertical line. Then bring your pencil down to the first line of the treble staff. Continue the curve across and to the right of the vertical line, bringing it up to the third line. Then swing your pencil across to the left and downward, ending a little below the second line of the staff. Your second treble staff line will be in the center of the lower circular part of the G clef you have just drawn. Go over the clefs in the heavy black of your felt nib pen. Make them as heavy as possible as they must dominate the chart. They should be as wide as the plain lines themselves, leaving the lettering uncovered.

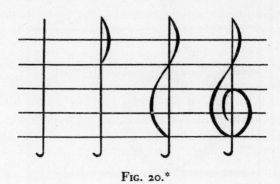

Marking the Spaces

Return the chart to its former position, the lettering on the bottom, the clefs now seen from a side view at the top. At the top edge of the chart, between the lines, write lightly with a pale crayon a small script letter, naming each space. At the bottom edge, still using the pale crayon, print a capital C at the bottom of the imaginary Middle C line.

Placement at the Keyboard

Return the chart to its position between the back of the keys and the wooden panel that extends behind the keyboard. Use a bit of easily removable masking tape to anchor the chart firmly to the wooden panel.

Alternate Placement

Make another chart identical with the above. Instead of placing it behind the piano keys, tape it to the wooden edge

* Drawing the treble clef, children grasp the entire treble staff.

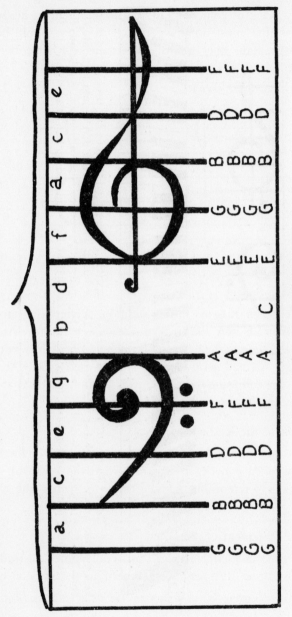

FIG. 21A. Staff Chart I.

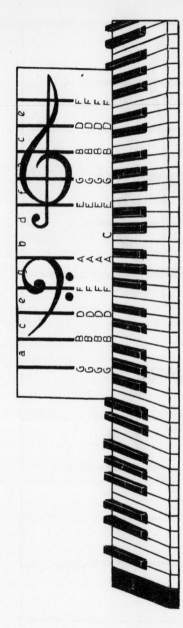

FIG. 21B. Staff Chart I (6" x 21", staff lines 1⅞" apart). To be placed between the back of the piano keys and the wooden panel that extends behind the keyboard. The lines of the staff should lead into the corresponding piano keys. A similar chart should be taped to the wooden edge in front of, and below, the corresponding piano keys. For a true image, stand at the left of keyboard and incline head slightly to the right.

in front of, and below, the keys, each line coinciding with (leading directly into) the center of its corresponding piano key.

STAFF CHART II

Make a somewhat similar but wider chart for wall use. Using posterboard eighteen inches by twenty-one inches (18″ × 21″) follow the instructions for the staff charts that go behind the piano keys, with this exception: After marking off the lines along the twenty-one inch side, omit the lettering until you have put in the clefs as well as the lines.

Then, holding the paper so that the clefs appear upright and the lines horizontal, continue each line to the right edge of the paper with a horizontal row of heavy black capital letters for the lines. Between the lines and at the right edge of the line-letters, a single small yellow letter can be used to indicate the name of each space (See Fig. 22). The alphabet progression may be readily seen.

This chart should hang on the wall or be placed upright in full sight during all the game sessions.

A duplicate chart can be used for relating the Grand Staff to the keyboard. Hold it like a tray at the front edge of the piano keys so that the Middle C location leads directly into the center of the Middle C piano key and the bottom line G leads into the second G from the left of the keyboard.

Always stand at the left of the keyboard when holding the chart as it is important to look at it from the bottom line up, to get the correct image.

The staff charts behind and below the piano keys show the Grand Staff lying on its side. This is not so disturbing as one might suppose, because the dominance of the clefs orients the onlooker who is thereby led to feel the relationship of the lines to the clefs. By standing at the left of the charts and looking

25

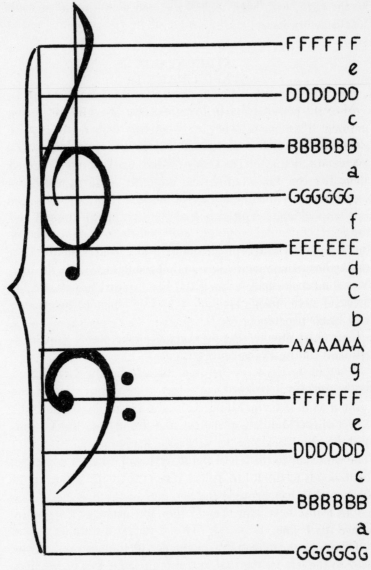

FIG. 22. Staff Chart II (18″ x 21″, staff lines 1⅞″ apart). To be used primarily as a wall hanging. May also be held like a tray in front of the corresponding piano keys.

to the right, with head slightly inclined to the right, one gets a satisfactory image.

STRIP STAFF

Another device for relating the musical playing field to the keys of the piano is a staff made of strips of cardboard or pipe cleaners. This can be used in conjunction with the charts just described.

MATERIALS NEEDED: Ten strips of dark cardboard (black, red, blue, or green, but all alike) cut a quarter of an inch wide, or less if possible, and about nine inches long. You will also need one strip of white cardboard (cover stock) of the same dimensions.

If you prefer to use pipe cleaners, you will need ten of some dark color to represent the staff lines and a single white one. You should also have enough additional pipe cleaners to make a G clef eleven inches high and a bass (F) clef six inches high; two black paper dots for the F clef. The clefs should be as narrow as possible, so they will not occupy too much space when they are laid on the keyboard.

Reviewing the Landmarks

Find Middle C, the white key to the left of the center Black Key Twins. The F line in the bass is below Middle C, therefore look for the Black Key Triplets immediately below Middle C. The white key to the left of the Black Key Triplets is the F that corresponds to the F line on the staff (the fourth line from the bottom that goes between the two dots of the bass clef). Now go up to the next white key to the right; that is G, the space above the F line.

Observing the relationship of this G to the Black Key Triplets, look to the left for the next lower set of Black Key Triplets. As we noted before, the white key to the left of the Black Key

27

Triplets is an F. Since it is the F which is an octave (eight notes) below the F line, it is located in the space below the bottom line G of the bass clef. Move up to the next white key on the right; this is the G that corresponds to the bottom line of the Grand Staff. (See Fig. 21B.)

Procedure

Depress this key (bottom line G). While you are holding the key down with one finger of your left hand, slip one end of a cardboard strip under the upright wood at the back edge of the piano keys to hold it. The rest of the strip, laid across the top of the key, will serve to mark G as the bottom line of the F clef. Skip the next white key to the right and continue to insert the strips for every *other* white key until five strips have been inserted. These represent the five lines of the bass clef.

Make an F clef out of wire or pipe cleaners or cut it out of black paper and lay it on top of the black piano keys so that it looks as if it began on the fourth strip up from the left or bottom. Put one paper dot on each white key on either side of the key that bears the fourth strip, (the F line).

Standing at the left of the piano and looking up the keyboard, i.e. looking to the right—you have superimposed the five lines and the clef of the bass staff. (Fig. 23)

The White Territory

Take your small strip of white paper, one-fourth of an inch wide. On it draw a short, thin, black line. The white strip will represent the Middle C and the small short black line on it will remind you that any note appearing on this line and therefore to be played on the corresponding piano key, must have the short black line through its center. Skip the white key above the top line strip of your bass staff. The white strip described above should be placed on the following white key. This is Middle C.

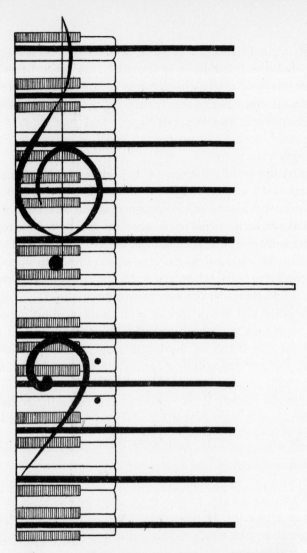

FIG. 23. Black strips inserted at corresponding piano keys represent the lines of the Grand Staff. The single white strip shows the Middle C line. For a satisfactory image when facing the keyboard, stand at the left of the lowest strip and incline head slightly to the right.

Bear in mind that the black keys of the piano have nothing to do with the black lines of the staff that we are building now with strips. In fact, for the present ignore the black keys of the piano and concentrate on the black lines of the staff and their relationship to the piano. If you find yourself confused by them, use strips of heavy stock or pipe cleaners of any dark color other than black.

After skipping the white key to the right of Middle C, begin to insert the five strips for the lines of the treble clef staff. Remember that after every insert of a strip you will skip a white key to the right to represent a space on the staff. When you have finished, place the long narrow G clef you have made out of several pipe cleaners or one long piece of wire. Be sure that the second strip of the five treble clef line strips runs through the center of the G clef's lower circular part.

CREATIVE APPLICATION

Take some music paper, or better still, make your own Grand Staff of eleven lines, erase the sixth one up from the bottom, draw your clefs, and write some notes. To begin with, write all quarter notes that get one swing each. Now go to the piano and play these notes.

Write a string of notes on lines in any order. Play this, using the chart as guide. Write a piece in space notes only and play this. Your music has no measure-lines as yet. The music for the church chants and the troubadour's songs in the Middle Ages had none either. In the next section you will be introduced to time signatures and measure-lines (which will advance you by at least a century!).

TELLING TIME

You look for a signature at the end of a letter. For a piece of music, look for the signature at the very beginning, to the right of each clef. First there may be a key signature that indicates the key in which the piece is written. To convey the first concepts necessary for music-learning through these play activities, you do not need to know about key signatures, because all the games (with only a few exceptions in the advanced section) are in the key of C which has no sharps or flats (symbols that mean certain notes are either raised or lowered in pitch).

If you have *no* key signature, the music is in the Key of C. If you have no sharps or flats, you use only the white keys on the piano and your staff chart will guide you.

TIME SIGNATURE

To the right of a key signature, if we had one, is the time signature. With no key signature, as in the key of C, the time signature comes directly after the clefs.

FIG. 24A.   4/4 time signature.

FIG. 24B.   Common time.

31

In some of these games we will use the time signatures three-four and four-four (3/4 and 4/4). The number three at the top of the fraction answers the question, "How many?" and the bottom number answers the question, "Of what kind of note?" ("Kind" in this instance refers to time-value.)

You know that one-fourth of a whole note is a quarter note, so the lower number in the time signature three-four (3/4) means a quarter note. When the top number says "three," the time signature is answering "Three" to the question, "How many?" and answering "Quarter notes" to the question, "What kind of note?" At this point, you are probably wondering, "In what?" The answer is, "In a measure."

MEASURE FOR MEASURE

A measure is also called a "bar" and a measure-line or bar-line is a vertical line that cuts through the horizontal lines of the staff. If the time signature said 3/4, within each measure or bar you could have three quarter notes or their equivalent in time-

(First Beat)

Fig. 25.

value, a dotted half note all by itself; or a half note and a quarter note, for example, which would also have a duration of three swings or beats and thus could make up your measure or bar. The completion of each bar has to be marked by the measure-line or bar-line. These measure-lines make it easier to

32

read and play music because the first beat in each measure is clearly indicated; it comes immediately after a measure-line.

Common Time or 4/4

Four-four as a time signature is common (many marches are in four-four time). Instead of writing 4/4 a composer often uses an abbreviation: the letter "c" to the right of the clefs; this "c" means common time or 4/4. (See Fig. 24B.)

FIG. 26. Common time measures (4/4 time). Vertical lines indicate bar-lines.

33

In analyzing this time signature ask yourself the two questions; considering the top of the fraction—"How many?"—"Four"; considering the bottom of the fraction—"Of what kind of note?"—"Quarter notes."

Four quarter notes would therefore make a measure; so would their equivalent time-value of four swings expressed in any of the other possible ways. One whole note would make a measure; or two half notes; or a dotted half note and a quarter; or a dotted half note and a pair of eighths; or a quarter, a half, and another quarter in any order, etc.

PRACTICAL APPLICATION

Creative Rhythms

Just as we experimented before with writing notes to indicate a succession of pitches, we will compose rhythmic patterns for four consecutive measures in three-four (3/4) time. A unit of four measures, called a four-measure "phrase" is common and is similar to a line of verse.

Composing a Waltz Tune

Cut out eight slips of paper, each three inches long. Make two creases so that you have three sections, each an inch long. (This is not to suggest that a 3/4 measure is three inches long and a 4/4 measure is four inches long, but graphically to depict the three swings represented by the time value of a 3/4 measure.) A triangle is a perfect demonstration in concrete form of a unit comprised of three even parts. Even saying the word "Tri-an-gle" will give you the sensation of three beats. Every time you say "triangle" you have finished a bar or measure in 3/4 time.

In each of the three sections created by the two creases, (on one of the slips) put a quarter note. On the next one, write a half note on the first section to the left, skip the second section

34

to indicate a continuing hold on that note, and put a quarter in the third section. Reverse this on another slip; have the quarter first and enter the half note on the second section. The third section remains blank and shows that a previous note is still sounding. Put a dotted half note on another slip at the left; the remaining two sections will be blank to show that the dotted half note is still sounding. Nothing more can go into that measure.

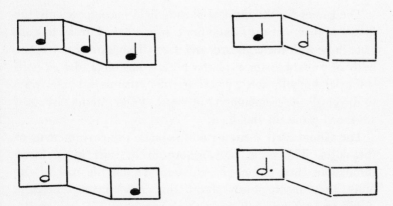

FIG. 27. 3/4 time measures. Each section of the strip indicates one beat.

Lay out four measures in a row with a match at the end of each one to act as a bar-line. If you have these notes all on one pitch you can make four *other* measures with the notes in the same or varying patterns but on different lines and spaces to indicate changes of pitch. Play your results on the piano using your chart as a guide.

Conducting in 3/4 Time

Form the slips into triangles. You can conduct a piece in 3/4 time by describing a triangle in the air for each measure. (See pp. 96–103.)

35

Try conducting the "Star Spangled Banner" in this manner. On the word "Oh," swing your right arm high above your head with a sweeping gesture. Then begin the first side of your imaginary triangle on the word "say." In conducting "My Country 'Tis of Thee," begin conducting directly on the first word, "My."

CONCLUSION

The games for the musical playing field encompass only the lines and spaces of the Grand Staff. If you have learned to associate these with the keyboard, and if you have learned to feel the beats or pulsations for a quarter note, a half note, dotted half, whole, and eighth notes, you have sufficient musical knowledge to direct all the elementary and many of the intermediate and advanced games in this book.

The Grand Staff is the natural habitat, the environment, of the notes. The notes move about in it, exist in it. Since throughout these games the children act out the part of the notes, they unconsciously absorb this environment. Therefore it will be your privilege not only to introduce children to the strange and fascinating world of music, but also to provide them with an experience that will whet their appetites for more knowledge and smooth their way to actual study.

2. *BACKGROUND FOR MORE ADVANCED GAMES*

Remove the music rack and prop the lid of a grand piano on its "stick" in order to get an unobstructed view of the inner life of the instrument.

As you lean over the piano and look into the depths behind the keyboard, you will see a continuous row of black or brown wooden objects resting on top of the strings. These are known as "dampers" and they stretch across nearly two-thirds of the instrument.

Each damper "belongs" to a separate key and rests on the strings that "belong" to each key.* Each damper rises a fraction of an inch above its neighbors when we depress the piano key that controls it, and returns to its lower position when the key is released.

It is not the purpose of this chapter to describe the technical functions of these dampers. They are merely referred to here because by watching them as we depress the white keys, for example, from Middle C to the C above, we get a clearer picture of half steps and whole steps between the adjacent notes of

---

* Do not be confused by the fact that a single damper covers three strings. This is because all these three strings are tuned alike and belong to one piano key.

the scale. The white keys from Middle C to the C above form a C major scale, but one can understand the structure of a major scale only in terms of half steps and whole steps.

When the twin black key "fingers" are pressed down, play the three white keys within that cluster so that all the keys of this group, black and white together, are all down. Now what do you see inside the piano? All the dampers that are attached to these keys spring up. They are all next to each other. The distance from one to another is called a "half step." Notice that even though three of the keys we are pressing down are white and two are black, inside the piano there is no color distinction.

If you play the three white keys and the two black keys in consecutive order, each of the five acting dampers would rise next to its immediate neighbor. In other words, white key C, black key to the right, white key D, black key to the right, and white key E, (played at the back edge near the wooden panel where you can see them more clearly in their successive order) would produce tones which are successively a half step or half tone apart.

From C to the black key directly on its right is a half step; this relationship is shown inside the piano by two raised dampers appearing side by side. If you play white key C, then skip the black key which follows, and play the next white key D, you will be playing two tones a whole step apart. In this case raised dampers are not next to each other—they are a whole step apart. As an analogy, think of a whole inch as opposed to a half inch. Here the distance is in tone vibrations.

To go back to the white key C, we speak of "raising it a half step" to C♯ which is the adjacent black key on its right. Now let us play the next white key D. We speak of "lowering it a half step" to D flat, when we merely go back and play the same black key that we just played for C♯. The black keys are named to express a relationship to neighboring white keys. For instance, as shown before, going up from C a half step, we play the black key to the right of it and call it C♯. Coming down from D a half step, play the same black key but call it D flat. (See p. 43 on chromatic scales.)

Now take the group of white keys in the orbit of the *three* black keys. If we press down the four white keys and the three black keys at the same time, we also have a procession of half steps, with all the active dampers rising side by side. Removing our fingers from the blacks, and playing only the white keys, we see inside the piano that the raised dampers are no longer close to each other; they are a whole step apart.

THE C MAJOR SCALE

We now have the stage set to introduce the C major scale. Without defining the word "scale" or "major," let us play all the white keys we have just been discussing.

First play (with the same fingers as before) the white keys, C, D, and E. Now with all the fingers of the right hand, beginning with thumb on F, play F, G, A, B, and, with the little finger that is now available, the next white key which is another C. You have played eight white keys.

Hold them all down at once so you can observe the inside action. The raised dampers touch only between the third and fourth and the seventh and eighth. This means that each of the tones is a whole step apart except those between the third and fourth and the seventh and eighth steps.

This series of eight tones in alphabetical order—C, D, E, F, G, A, B, and the return to one of the same name as the beginning C is a major scale without sharps or flats. It can therefore be played entirely on the white keys of the piano. Each is a whole step apart from the other except the white keys E and F and the white keys B and C. Notice on the keyboard that there exists no black key between these pairs of notes. Yet inside the piano, when these keys have been sounded, two dampers spring

39

up side by side indicating a half step between E and F; the same is true of adjacent white keys B and C.

Major scales may differ in pitch if they start on other notes, but they are all similar in their arrangement of whole and half steps. When beginnning a major scale on another note, sharps or flats must be used in order to produce the same arrangement of dampers that can be seen when the white keys from one C to the next higher C are played. Beginning on any key on the piano, black or white, it is possible to reproduce this formula: Starting note,* whole step, whole step, half step; whole, whole, whole, and half, which last note lands us on a note of the same name as the starting note.

The distance between these two notes of the same name is called an octave, which comes from the Latin word meaning "eight." From C to C in the musical alphabet, one uses the seven different alphabet names and then repeats the first one. Each of these alphabet-named notes is called a degree or a step in the scale. (The lines and spaces of the staff are sometimes called staff degrees.) Tones in alphabetical order are said to be in "step-wise progression." From a line of the staff to its adjacent space to the next line, and then to the next space would be a "step-wise progression" up the staff.

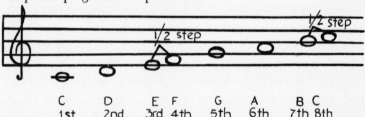

FIG. 28. C major scale. Starting point (C) is called the key-note or tonic. The eighth degree is also the tonic.

So a major scale could be defined as a succession of eight tones in step-wise progression from any note to its octave; a

* Also called keynote or tonic.

40

whole step appearing between the first and second degrees, the second and third degrees, the fourth and fifth degrees, the fifth and sixth degrees, the sixth and seventh degrees, and only a half step between the third and fourth degrees and the seventh and eighth, reckoning upwards from the starting or keynote. The eight tones are each a whole step apart except the third and fourth, and seventh and eighth, which are a half step apart.

If one began a major scale on G and continued upward in step-wise progression (alphabetically—line to space to line, etc.) the sequence of notes would fulfill our requirement for the arrangement of whole steps and half steps only until we came to the sixth step E. We have already noted that there is a natural half step between the two white keys E and F; however we need

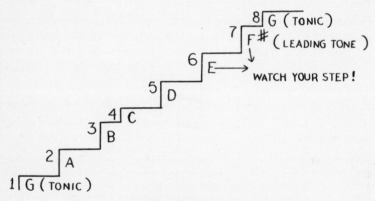

FIG. 29. Ladder design, G major shown.

a *whole* step between the sixth and seventh degrees. This seventh step is called the leading tone in the scale or key, because by virtue of this half step relationship, it has a strong pull toward the keynote, the eighth degree which has the same name as the first degree.

We can remedy this situation by raising the seventh step to F♯. Now all our requirements are met. There is a whole step

41

now from E to F♯ (our sixth to seventh degree) and also a half step from Leading Tone F♯ to G (our seventh to eighth step).

FIG. 30.

The sharp is put on the F line in the key signature (to the right of each clef) and it guarantees that all F's will be F♯'s, unless specifically cancelled by a "natural." This symbol is then written in front of any F that is not to be one of the taken-for-granted F♯'s in the key.

FIG. 31. A natural cancels a sharp or flat.

The scale or key is called G major and like all sharp signature keys is named for the degree directly above the signature's last sharp, which falls on the leading tone. Since F♯ is our seventh degree, the key takes its name from the eighth degree G, which is the same in name as the first note (starting point or tonic).

(The word "scale" as distinguished from the word "key" refers only to a formal arrangement of tones in ascending or descending order of pitch; the word "key" refers to the free use of these very same tones in any order, as the basis for a musical composition.)

There are other types of scales (minor scales, whole tone scales, etc.) but this book touches only on the major scale and on the chromatic scale. The chromatic scale consists of a series of half steps from C to C. All the raised dampers will be close to each other as they spring up when all the half steps from C to C are held down at once.

The custom is to use the sharp symbols going up the chromatic scale—C, C sharp, D, D sharp, E, F, F sharp, etc. Coming down from the higher C to the lower C, one uses the flat symbols, C, B, B flat, etc.

Playing near the wooden panel at the back edge of the keyboard, name each key from C to C. Do not use the word "sharp" or "flat" in the chromatic scale when going from white key E to white key F or from white key B to white key C (or descending F to E, or C to B) since these white keys are a natural half step apart.

C to C♯ is also a half step apart but the black keys do not have alphabet names of their own, but rather assume names that express a relationship to neighboring white keys, as mentioned on pp. 216–218.

With the assimilation of this knowledge the leader is equipped to direct any of the intermediate and advanced games.

3. *NECESSARY EQUIPMENT*

THE PLAYING FIELD

Heading the list of necessary equipment is the playing field itself.

On an outdoor playground, the ten black lines should be painted at least a foot apart except between the fifth line or top of the bass clef and the first line of the treble clef where the space should be doubled. This allows for the Magic C line even though it is imaginary.

The clefs must be accurately drawn because most of the learning matter involves the G line which runs through the center of the round part of the treble clef (G clef) and the F line (fourth line) which runs between the two dots of the bass (F clef).

The names of the F clef and the G clef are derived from the function they perform of designating the F line and the G line. These, as well as the magic Middle C line, become mental landmarks which help to fix all other staff relationships in the first stage of unconsciously absorbing the entire staff.

Often public playgrounds have shuffleboard or handball courts laid out in yellow paint. Black is preferable for the musical playing field, since it more closely resembles printed music, but other colors can be used if necessary.

Where the music staff cannot be painted on the cement, it may be represented by black tapes stuck to the floor. The clefs may be cut out and also taped to the floor or even shaped out of the tape itself. Naturally, this is a makeshift, as it is far more satisfactory to have the musical playing field permanently painted on the ground area. However, using black tape to lay out various game courts has always been standard practice in gymnasiums.

Any room-sized linoleum rug can be painted over several times until it appears completely white. The musical game court of lines and clefs can then be painted in glossy black, and the entire surface given two coats of transparent shellac for protection. It is wise to ask the children to play on it in their stocking feet, as they do in many dance groups.

It is possible to buy white linoleum in narrow widths. In this case, make the staff in two sections, one for the treble and the other for the five lines of the bass section, the meeting of the two forming the Middle C. The magic Middle C line is now a crack between the two pieces.

In this way one can get as wide a staff as one desires, although the height now is dictated by the width in which the white linoleum is sold.

Church rooms and all-purpose rooms in community centers often require that all materials used be put out of sight or removed after each session. In that case the musical playing field can be painted on white oilcloth in two sections, one for the bass and one for the treble. A large piece of canvas in one piece also makes an adequate game court that can be rolled up. "Mystic" tape can be used at the corners to anchor the game court to the floor.

Experiment with the new materials coming on the market, foam rubber on one side and a cloth surface on the other side. These are sold for table lining pads and mattress covers. (Goodrich makes such a mattress cover.) This material demands that players wear no shoes, only socks. Curon, a Curtiss-Wright product, may be painted white on its thread-covered side. Only flat paint is recommended for Curon.

Oilcloth, canvas, and cotton-backed foam-rubber-like materials have the advantage of being easily rolled up. The author used one for a whole year which, together with all her symbols, costumes, cards, charts, and other materials, fitted into two boxes such as department stores use for packing coats. After every music-learning session, everything went into the boxes until the following week and the room returned to its everyday routine as the office of a settlement school director.

Finding a Place

Finding a large play area indoors is often a problem. Gymnasiums or school cafeterias which lead a multiple life usually have a piano and could furnish an ideal indoor area for these games. Where the gymnasium is constantly in use for athletics, the stage usually found at one end of the gym or cafeteria or even the regular auditorium stage can be curtained off. A list of games suitable for small rooms and fairly large rooms as well as those that require a real playground is provided in the Appendix. Basement or attic "rumpus rooms" in homes lend themselves to this purpose.

SYMBOLS

Large cutout notes and other musical symbols, rests, clefs, sharps, flats, naturals, and numerals for time signatures are essential. If possible, it would be most helpful to have several sets of notes—quarters, half notes, dotted half notes, whole notes, a pair of eighths joined together—cut out of thin plywood with a jigsaw and painted black. These resist tearing by the children in such games as Musical Chairs where there is competition in getting to the notes. Otherwise, they can be made of heavy black paper (cover stock). Small cutout notes may be cut from black construction paper by the children themselves. Other colors may be used by the younger children, such as red, green, and blue.

Pipe-cleaner Notes

Pipe cleaners can be used to make the notes and symbols. A simple twist will make the circle attached to the stick of the half note and the simple oval or circle for the whole note. To make the solid head for a quarter or eighth note, start with one tip and wind it into a firm coil, using up half of the pipe cleaner. The unwound remainder serves as the stem.

Dots

When making a dotted half note from any material, simply attach a black paper dot to the half note by means of Scotch tape. Cover the sticky side that is left exposed with more Scotch tape. In the same way, add dots to the bass clef, fixing them so that the fourth line of the bass staff F will pass between the two dots.

COSTUMES AND CARDS

Children love to play Let's Pretend and Let's Dress Up. Wearing the large paper symbols makes the child feel that he is actually personifying a note or other musical symbol.

The arm is thrust through the hole of the half, the dotted half, and the whole note, so that these notes are worn over the shoulder. They can also be worn on the head as a crown or beret.

The quarter note with its solid head should be attached to the body by means of black elastic tape or cord which also acts as the symbol of a staff-line cutting through the center of the note-head. A note cannot be said to be on a line unless the line

47

cuts through the center of its head. To be on a space the head of the note should be clear of any line. Thus the black tape can be used to illustrate the placing of a note on a line or space. Two lines, or tapes, one above the head of the note, and one below, would show a note in a space.

Note Cards

A set of twenty-one cards is needed to show a single note on each of the lines and spaces of the Grand Staff, which has ten visible lines and the magic Middle C line, all eleven of which create ten spaces. Each card is to show the entire Grand Staff but only one note. These notes should be of different time-value: quarter, half, dotted half, and whole notes.

These cards should be the standard construction paper size, $9'' \times 12''$ and should be strung at the top corners with elastic cord to permit their being easily slipped on and off.

Note Hats

Gay party hats make us think of a party as much as ice cream and cake. Each child should have his own party hat for these music-learning games.

A triangular piece of brightly colored crepe paper can be taped at the two opposite corners to make a simple crown-like hat. Small cutout note symbols are then attached with a paper clip at the top. If a note on a specific line or space is required, a note card may be substituted for the cutout.

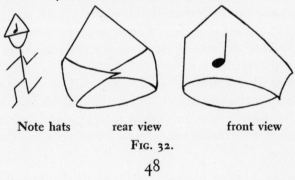

Note hats   rear view   front view
Fig. 32.

48

These note hats are recommended for the more strenuous games such as At the Bridge and various tag games, where the note costumes might be damaged.

Less colorful but sometimes more available are paper bags that the children can collect after a shopping trip with Mother. Each child should mark his hat with his name so that he may always wear his own.

Beanbag Notes

Small black oval beanbags to represent notes are needed for a number of the games. There should be supplies of construction paper, drawer-lining paper, crepe paper, cardboard, crayons, scissors, Scotch tape, masking tape, pencils, pipe cleaners, yardsticks, etc.

For outdoor use a megaphone and a whistle are invaluable to the leader.

A MUSICAL INSTRUMENT FOR OUTDOORS

Indoors, the piano is the perfect instrument for correlating the lines and spaces of the staff with their equivalent sounds. But what about an instrument for the outdoor musical playing field? A pitch pipe, a set of bells, or a toy xylophone will provide the sounds only for the treble clef. Obviously we need an instrument that will furnish the pitch for each of the lines and spaces of the staff.

The Autoharp in its original form will furnish the corresponding tones for the notes of the staff from the F line in the bass to the top F line in the treble as well as the bottom bass line G. Five tones that we need are missing. However, anyone who is experimental and adventurous can join with the author in creating an exciting new instrument that is indispensable for the outdoor musical playing field games merely by retuning and otherwise converting an Autoharp for the sole purpose of making audible every line and space on the playing field.

The author has successfully retuned the strings that are already on the Autoharp by matching the pitch of the Autoharp's bottom string to the second G below Middle C on the piano. (This is the pitch it was originally meant to have.) The next string will have to be tuned down much lower to match in pitch the white key directly above this G. It must correspond with the second A below Middle C. The third string will be tuned down to sound like the next white key B, and so on, going through all the white keys from the one representing the bottom bass line G to the white piano key representing the top treble line F. All the strings (except the two top strings on the Autoharp which are superfluous for our purpose) will be the pitch equivalent of all the lines and spaces of the staff.

The author suggests that you keep this converted Autoharp for the musical playing field games and not expect to tune it back for its original use in accompanying songs, etc. Use other Autoharps for this purpose if you wish, but since the preparation of this instrument for the musical playing field requires great care in tuning and a special chart under the strings, reserve it for the sole purpose of integrating sounds with the lines and spaces of the staff. If you are doubtful about being able to retune the instrument, ask a friend with a keen ear and musical training to help you. With practice you will be able to keep it in tune yourself if you can "carry a tune," as they say. In a short time, the children too will be at home with it and will be able to come up to it and pluck the right string for a specific line or space.

Now take a narrow strip of white paper, approximately 4½″ × 7½″. Draw eleven lines about five-eighths of an inch apart. (Measure distance from the bottom string to the third string.) Draw these lines lightly in pencil at first, starting close to the bottom of your paper strip. The lines correspond with every other string on the Autoharp.

Erase the sixth line from the bottom as this will be the location of Middle C. Slip the chart beneath the strings of the

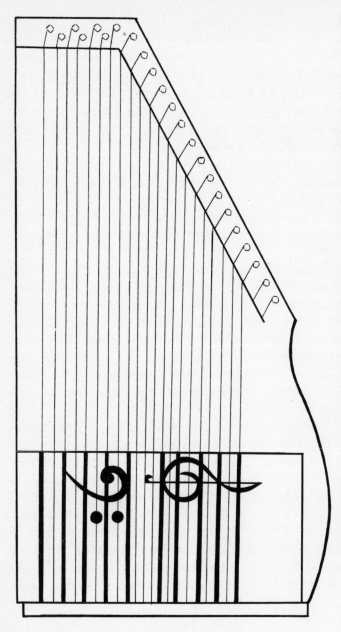

FIG. 33. Musical instrument for the outdoors. Shown here are only the essential parts of an Autoharp retuned for musical playing field games.

Autoharp over the existing chart to check for accuracy. Draw in the two clefs, starting with the F clef (bass) on the fourth line from the bottom and planning the G clef so that the second treble line G will go through the center of the round part. (See Fig. 20.) Make the F clef dots heavy and blacken the lines of the staff with a felt nib marking pen. This will focus the attention on the heavy black lines of the paper staff when the chart is replaced beneath the strings.

Be sure the heavy lines are under their pitch-equivalent strings and then tape the chart, top and bottom, to the wooden body of the Autoharp.

There is now a string above each heavy line of the new paper staff and there is also a string for each white space *between* the heavy lines.

This means that there is now a perfect correlation—a direct correspondence—between the instrument and the musical playing field, between the instrument and printed music. Any song without sharps or flats in the signature (in C major) can be played merely by plucking the lines and spaces indicated by the notes in the song.

Remember: Think of the strings above the heavy black lines as "lines" and the strings without a black line under them as "spaces."

You now have an instrument that is not only easily carried outdoors but one that will furnish the pitch that should be associated and fused with every line and space of the Grand Staff. Not only will you be able to play it, but the children will be able to pluck the string that will give them the sound of any line or space on which they have landed a beanbag or themselves. It can be used to advantage in every game set forth in this book. Because of its coordination of the senses of hearing, seeing, and touching, a true concept of the meaning of the musical staff will form and remain as a basis for reading music.

4. GENERAL SUGGESTIONS

1. Explain each game thoroughly before attempting to play it. A large staff drawn on cardboard on which to move small toy figures can serve to give an animated and vivid demonstration of the formation and activity in each game.

2. Half-hour sessions are ideal for the five- and six-year-old groups, forty-five minutes for the older ones.

Ideally, two people should be in charge—one to direct the games, the other to play the necessary incidental music at the piano. The first needs only the background absorbed from the orientation and preparation chapters; the other needs only enough piano technique to play the simple songs listed in the appendix and the musical examples in this book.

3. With the exception of Pussy in the Corner which uses only four players at a time, most of the other games can be adapted to groups of eight to sixteen players. Many of the games and activities can also be used by the large classes that exist in the public schools.*

* The Play Schools Association in a summer recreational program for underprivileged children tried out some of these games on the roof of a public school. The older children drew the musical playing field and the younger children played on it. Both gained in knowledge.

Do not hesitate to use the services of both young and old in making some of your "props" as there is music-learning in the preparations as well as in the games themselves.

4. Every mother who has ever had a birthday party for her child knows that there is usually someone who will not enter wholeheartedly into all the festivities. In a large class or group, there is often someone who lives up to his reputation as a "behavior problem." By giving the uncooperative one some "busy" work such as cutting out the note symbol costumes or making the note hats, you can keep him from spoiling the fun for the others and at the same time provide him with an opportunity to learn independently and still make a real contribution to the whole group. Having established himself as a useful member of society, he inevitably acquires an almost proprietary interest in the proceedings and willingly participates with the others.

5. Glancing at Fig. 35, p. 58, one sees, to the left of the clefs, a brace that joins the treble and bass staves. This brace is an integral part of the Grand Staff. See also Fig. 9, on page 11 and Fig. 22, on page 26. However, because of space or labor limitations, it may be omitted from the musical playing field, since the children need only the lines, spaces, and clefs for their play area.

Seeing the brace on the staff charts constantly, children can imagine it on the playing field. Occasionally, they should place a large cutout brace or a long black tape curled like a brace to the left of the bass and treble staves as a reminder of its existence.

II

Games Section

1. ELEMENTARY GAMES

FIG. 34. Dancing on the lines and spaces.

ACQUAINTANCE WITH THE LINES AND SPACES

MUSIC: Singing to the tune of "How Do You Do, My Partner?"

EQUIPMENT: None, other than the playing field.

NUMBER OF CHILDREN: Any number.

GAME: Two children, both on the lowest line, stand side by side, facing the top of the staff. They sing:

> How do you do, my partner?
> How do you do today?
> Will you dance on this bottom line?
> I will show you the way.

57

FIG. 35. "How Do You Do, My Partner?"

Holding hands, they side-skip across the staff, staying on the line.

Two new children come up to the staff and stand side by side in the first white space. They sing: "How do you do," etc. except that in the third line of the verse they sing, "Will you dance in the first space? I will show you the way."

Each couple goes through the same routine, except that they go to the next higher line or space. In the song, they specify which line or space. The lines are designated: first, second, third, fourth, and fifth for each staff, starting from the bottom line of first the bass and then the treble. At Middle C, they sing, "Will you dance on the Middle C line?" The spaces above and below Middle C are referred to thus: "Will you dance on the space below Middle C?"—or "above Middle C?" A bit awkward fitting that many syllables into the line, but it makes the children aware of these spaces.

This is a difficult area for children to grasp visually because the Middle C line is imaginary and does not provide the needed visual anchorage to mark the spaces on either side of it distinctly. Young children are intrigued by the idea that the Middle C line is "magic" and that a little bit of this magic line "pops out" and turns black like the other lines only when a note is placed on it. One telephone-conscious child had her own theory: "Middle C has its own private line." Another said, "All the other notes on the staff have something to sit on, but Middle C has to bring his own bench."

LEARNING GOAL: Discrimination between lines and spaces; spatial relationships on the staff through recognition of first, second, third, fourth, and fifth lines of each clef as well as recognition of first, second, third, and fourth spaces in each clef and the space above and below Middle C.

ALL SET FOR SCHOOL

EQUIPMENT: Musical instrument, indoors, preferably a piano, with Staff Chart I (Fig. 21B) inserted behind keyboard; outdoors a specially tuned Autoharp. (See pp. 23, 24, 51.)

FORMATION: Players stand below the staff in a horizontal line facing the lines of the staff.

GAME: The leader sounds the tone corresponding to the bottom line of the bass staff. She explains, "When you hear this sound— the sound of the lowest line in the bass, run to that line and pretend to shine your shoes."

Next, the leader plays the sound corresponding to the fifth or top line of the bass staff. "When you hear this, run to the fifth line and pretend to comb your hair."

For practice, she plays first the lower sound, then the higher. The children are to follow the tones by running to the corresponding staff location and going through the appropriate gestures, either shining their shoes or combing their hair. The leader then plays the sound of the third line, saying, "When you hear the sound of the middle line, buckle your belt."

All three activities are then signaled only by sound: shoe-shining on the bottom line, belt-buckling on the middle line, and hair-combing on the top line. First one to arrive at each appropriate line and to groom himself properly earns a point. Five points take him to the top of his class. He may stand at the extreme left of the line of children nearest to the clefs.

At another session, the leader begins the game in the same

way. After the children prove that they can relate the three tones to the suggested activities and to the bass staff, she says, "We have forgotten something. Your knees could use a little scrubbing." This action must take place on the second line from the bottom of the staff as its corresponding sound is played.

One more detail needs attention. Clothes need brushing. "Brush your shoulders" says the leader as she plays the fourth line F in the bass clef, the line that runs between the two dots of the F clef. (Point this out often.)

All Set for School is now a complete routine. The children run to whichever line is indicated by the sound, and respond with a corresponding action and staff location.

The same lines on the treble staff are worked out in the same way, starting with the bottom line of the treble alternated with the top line. Next the treble middle line is added and finally the G line, the second on the treble staff, and the fourth line also. The children can now sing "Shine your shoes" or "Scrub your knees" to the correct pitch as the treble clef lies within their voice range.

LEARNING GOALS: Space relationships on the staff; personal association of staff line to a corresponding location on the body; ear training, and visual training.

ALPHABET SOUP (A Counting-Out Game)

Counting-out is a traditional way of choosing the chief players in a game, usually accompanied by nonsense syllables uttered by one child who goes from player to player, hitting everyone's held-out fist with his own. Last one hit is IT. Sometimes the counting-out is as much fun as the game which it precedes. Alphabet Soup is based on these counting-out diversions. Besides offering a bit of amusement, it introduces the musical alphabet.

In Alphabet Soup, the first one to call out, "ABCDEFGA" is

the leader or the one who will count out. Each child holds out his right fist. The leader whom we shall call Cook fits his own right fist on that of each player in turn, and together they go through the motions of stirring soup. Their purpose is to find a certain alphabet-shaped noodle.

FIG. 36.

As they stir, first player says "A"; the other players after him go through the remainder of the musical alphabet remembering that after a letter G comes an A. Each one stirs the soup with the Cook, and names the next letter in the seven-letter alphabet. Two complete rounds of the alphabet are gone through; the "A" at the start of the third round is IT.

ALPHABET SOUP (Second Helping)

In this version for a more experienced group, the alphabet letters form a diagonal row up the staff, starting with the first space A (above the bottom line in the bass) and occupying each successive line and space.

Cook goes from player to player, placing his fist on top of that of each player and going through the soup-stirring gesture as he stops to look for the next alphabet letter.

Beginning with A, each player tells what letter he sees. This is the name of his line or space.

Since the players occupy successive lines and spaces on the music-staff playing field, it will be immediately evident that the alphabet goes forward as the leader goes up the staff and that after a space named G there comes a line named A and after a line named G comes a space named A.

Cook goes up the staff twice the same way. Each alphabet noodle is expected to remember his name. After stirring the top pot of soup, Cook starts to come down the staff. Anyone who fumbles or forgets his name becomes IT for any game described in this book, because this game is really part of the counting-out process.

Naturally, if to be IT in a specific game is a special honor it wouldn't be fair to award it to someone who had made a mistake. In this case, the coveted prize would go to the next player.

LEARNING GOAL: Familiarity with the musical alphabet, particularly the progression from G to A.

AMONG FRIENDS

EQUIPMENT: Black elastic cord, large cutout symbols, drums, and other instruments if desired.

MUSIC: Singing to the tune of "Oh, Do You Know the Muffin Man?"

NUMBER OF PLAYERS: The more the merrier.

COSTUMES: If there is a large number of children, they are divided into Quarter Notes, Half Notes, Dotted Half Notes, and Whole Notes. They wear their symbols as costumes. The paper notes are held on by an elastic cord tied around the waists of the players. The cord represents a line going through the note as it does on printed music. If there are only four or five children, only one is a Quarter Note and each of the others represents a different time-value. Note hats may also be worn.

FORMATION: The children form a circle, one child in the center, as they begin to sing. The center player brings others dressed like himself within the circle. Between verses, marching and acting out time-values may break up the circle, but it re-forms at the beginning of each new time-value.

GAMES: Everyone sings and marches around in a circle, holding hands. One Quarter-note child stands in the center.

> Oh, do you know the Quarter Note,
> The Quarter Note, the Quarter Note?
> Oh, do you know the Quarter Note,
> That lives in Music-Land?

FIG. 37. "Oh, Do You Know the Quarter Note?"

The center Quarter Note now leads any other Quarter Notes into the center, if the group is large; otherwise he remains alone while all continue to sing:

> Oh, yes, we know the Quarter Note,
> The Quarter Note, the Quarter Note,
> Oh, yes, we know the Quarter Note
> That lives in Music-Land.

After this verse is sung, they all sing just the first line of it so that each syllable gets one swing. Then they march as they swing both arms to each syllable, taking one step to each swing.

The step, the swing, and the sung syllable are thus synchronized.

At the end of a short march around the staff (or just around a room) the circle re-forms, the Quarter Notes are back in the circle. Everyone sings:

> Oh, do you know the Half Note,
> The Half Note, the Half-Note,
> Oh, do you know the Half Note,
> That lives in Music-Land?

As before, the single Half Note can bring the other Half Notes into the center and the rest continue to go around singing the second half of the half-note verse.

> Oh, yes, we know the Half Note,
> The Half Note, the Half Note,
> Oh, yes, we know the Half Note
> That lives in Music-Land.

It is amusing to distort the rhythm of the song's first line at this point so that every syllable is held for a half note. To this, each child swings both arms backward and forward like the ropes of a swing. Hold each syllable for two swings.

> Oh - - do - - you - - know - - the - - Half - - note - -? *

Proceed in similar manner with the Dotted Half Note:

> Oh, do you know the Dotted Half,
> The Dotted Half, the Dotted Half?
> Oh, do you know the Dotted Half
> That lives in Music-Land?
>
> Oh, yes, we know, etc.

* Dashes represent arm swings accompanying each prolonged word.

For the Dotted Half Note, sing the first four words of the song again;

Oh - - - do - - - you - - - know - - -?

(Swing back, forward, back for *each* syllable.)

Do the same with the Whole Note: "Oh, do you know the Whole Note?" etc.

Finish it up with the slow singing of "Oh - - - - do - - - - you - - - - know - - - -?" each syllable becoming a whole note, and therefore receiving four swings: back, forward, back, forward. Step on the first backward swing of the arms; wait during the remaining three swings.

Variation

Four sections or blocks can be chalked on the playing area and each time-value stands in as many as he is entitled to, each section representing one beat.

Only as many Notes can come into the center of the ring as can be accommodated there.

For example, only four Quarters may enter; only two Half Notes may enter. Each of the latter stands in two blocks. Only one Dotted Half may enter, leaving one block empty.

After the Dotted Half verses are sung and the marching and swinging coordinations are worked out, the Dotted Half Note may choose a Quarter to stand beside him.

Variation

The original Quarter Note within the circle must choose a definite line on which to stand and any other time-value children that he brings into the center must stand on the same line with him.

The children remaining in the circle sing accordingly, for example:

Oh, do you know the Quarter Note, the Quarter Note, etc.
   That lives on the second line in the bass?

As the game proceeds, each new time-value chooses a new staff location for himself and any of his partners. Each new staff location is described in the last line of each verse that is sung.

LEARNING GOALS: Recognition of symbols, development of co-ordination, and intense concentration through the multiple interpretation of time-values.

Variation

The game can be more exciting if the Notes are not chosen to enter the center of the ring but run in to occupy the sections. The unlucky ones return to the ring each time. Only one measureful can be housed within the circle.

LEARNING GOAL: This variation has its own learning goal: the measure concept.

AS WE HAVE DONE BEFORE

MUSIC: Sing the words to the tune of "Go in and Out the Window."

NUMBER OF CHILDREN: Between six and twelve, preferably twelve in order to cover the whole staff.

FORMATION: There are two formations. In the first, the players form a horizontal line on the lowest space of the staff, facing toward the top. In the second, they arrange themselves in a diagonal row up the staff, each raising an arm to join hands with his neighbor, forming a series of arches.

GAME: Players take positions in a horizontal line on the lowest space and hold hands as they walk up the staff, stepping only on the spaces and singing:

> Go up the staff in spaces,
> Go up the staff in spaces,

66

Go up the staff in spaces,
As we have done before.

FIG. 38.   "Go Up the Staff in Spaces."

Upon reaching the top line of the entire staff, they remain facing as they started, but they walk down backwards, still holding hands and singing:

Go down the staff in spaces, etc.

As they all reach the bottom G line, one child at the left end of the line steps aside as the rest arrange themselves diagonally in a row up the staff, all standing only in the spaces. The single child now weaves in and out of the arches made by the other children as they raise their arms and hold hands. They sing:

Go in between the spaces,
Go in between the spaces, etc.

The child going in and out steps *only on the lines* as he goes in between the spaces.

When he finishes, he joins the row of children at the right end, and they all re-form into a horizontal row across the bottom line. They proceed up again, this time stepping *only on lines*, singing:

Go up the staff on lines, etc.

67

They go down stepping backward and singing:

Go down the staff on lines, etc.

FIG. 39. **Go up the staff in spaces, in and out of the arches.**

Again the child on the left end of the line detaches himself from the others, who again arrange themselves diagonally up the staff. The single child weaves in and out of the arches as all sing:

Go in between the lines, etc.

In order to do this, he must step only on spaces. If he accidentally steps on a line, someone else takes his turn.

The new leader now sings:

Now follow me to the G clef
(repeat twice)
And we'll walk along the G line.

(Or hop along, run, etc. or other activity. Repeated notes on this line, all G's, can be played on the piano. All match actions to the song.)

Next:

> Now follow me to the F clef, etc.
> And we'll (walk) along the F line.
> Now follow me to Middle C, etc.
> And we'll (hop) along this magic line.

(Vary the words and action to "tiptoe on," "slide along," etc.)
The others follow as the leader acts out his song. The action is always from left to right across the staff on the last-named three lines. New leaders may be chosen for each of these lines.

LEARNING GOALS: Discrimination between lines and spaces. Recognition of G clef, G line, F clef, and F line, two important landmarks, as well as the magic Middle C line. This game stimulates alertness in reading up and down the staff as well as across the lines.

FIG. 40. At the Bridge.

AT THE BRIDGE

EQUIPMENT: Small symbols or note hats worn by the children.

GAME: Any number may play. Two players leave the group to decide between themselves which shall be the Bass Clef and which the Treble Clef. No one must know their decision. The other children form a circle holding hands. One Clef enters the circle, the other stands opposite him on the outside of the circle. The two make an arch with their arms. Now they begin to sing. The players in the circle drop their hands and turn right to march through the arch made by the Clefs.

Whole Notes, Half Notes,
Quarters, Eighth Notes,
Dotted Half Notes, too.
Many a note have we let go
Because we wanted you.

FIG. 41. "Whole Notes, Half Notes, Quarters."

On reaching the word "you," the Clef arch snaps down and captures a member of the circle. The Clefs hold him and rock him the number of times indicated by his time-value costume or note hat: once for a Quarter, twice for a Half, three times for a Dotted Half, and four times for a Whole Note. A single Eighth Note does not get rocked at all.

The captive is taken away from the others and asked in a whisper which Clef he would like to join, the Bass or the Treble. When he has chosen, he is told to keep the secret and stand behind the Clef he has chosen.

70

When all are caught and have chosen their sides, the Clefs collect the costumes of their captives and take their position on the Clef they represent. Each player grasps the waist of the player in front of him and there is a tug of war.

LEARNING GOAL: Familiarity with time-value symbols.

AT THE MARKET

Each player is fitted out with a price tag around his neck. These are time-value cards bearing the sign of a quarter, a half, a dotted half, or a whole note. The cards have elastic thread or cord through holes in the corners. (Reinforcements are advised for the holes.)

The Buyer comes up to the Seller, who squats with his hands clasping his knees. Buyer asks the price of a Note. Seller consults price tag and explains the price by specifying the number of swings the time-value is worth. If the Buyer is interested, Buyer and Seller take the Note by each arm and swing him the appropriate number of swings. If he loses his balance he is rejected.

Dialogue between Buyer and Seller is developed about the merits of each Note, whether it is a nice plump Half Note or perhaps too thin a Quarter Note, etc. The swinging is to determine whether he is "just right."

LEARNING GOAL: Familiarity with time-value symbols.

B-C-D, RUN FROM ME

Preliminaries

Before starting the game, there should be a short discussion of what notes lie in the White Territory between the bass and treble clefs, which we will call B-C-D Land.

Having reviewed B as the space below Middle C, C itself, and D as the space above Middle C, the game will be played in three "innings," once for catching a B, then for catching a C, and finally D. Before playing the first round for B, review the places of all the B's on the staff. For the remaining two rounds, review the C's, and then all the D's.

GAME: The children make a circle around the B-C-D Land. All try to keep out of this forbidden area themselves, but try to make their fellow players touch or get dragged into it as in the game of Poison, an old folk game. We don't want any unpleasant associations with this section so let us try to think of it as "forbidden."

The first one to be pulled or pushed into the White Territory or B-C-D Land, becomes B. As soon as the players cry, "You're B!" or "Mary is B," they run away from B, and if they can touch or land on any B in the Grand Staff, they are safe. Anyone caught will stand off to the side of the staff but still on B, if one imagines the lines and spaces extended indefinitely. These players may aid in the capture of C in the next round.

The circle re-forms around the B-C-D Land, and whoever gets pulled in becomes C. He is aided by the B's caught in the last round. Any member of the circle able to reach C on the staff is safe. Those caught stand at the side on a line that would be an extension of Middle C. They and the others caught before will try to catch the D's. If the group is small, they should not stand apart from the circle but should pay a forfeit, such as having to walk in some odd way along all the lines and spaces bearing their name.

The game continues in the same fashion except that the first person pulled into the B-C-D Land becomes a D. After this round, the game ends or begins all over again.

Even a young and inexperienced group can enjoy playing this game despite the fact that it demands that they become familiar with other B's, C's, and D's on the staff besides the B, C, and D in the White Territory. Use pieces of brightly colored Mystic or masking tape to stick on the "safe" lines near the edge of the staff. The name of the line or space can be written on the tape.

When the children have a chance to hear several B's sounded together, they will recognize a specially close relationship.

LEARNING GOAL: Concept that there is more than one B, C, or D on the staff. Complete mastery of the three notes in the section between the bass and treble. Ear training for the interval of an octave, the distance of eight staff degrees from one note to another of the same name.

BAIT THE B-C-D (An Adaptation of the Folk Game "Baste the Bear")

Middle C sits on a stick or strip of black cardboard. B and D are his "keepers." The other children stand in a circle around the outside edge of the staff. B and D are not allowed to move out of their B-C-D territory. They hold hands with Middle C, B on his left, D on his right. B stands a little below C, D a little above.

No one may touch Middle C until B and D call out:

> Middle C, Middle C
> Sitting on a line!
> If you dare to touch him
> You will have to pay a fine!

The circle players try to touch Middle C without being touched by him, or B, or D, who try to protect their charge. Anyone touched by Middle C trades places with him; anyone touched by either of Middle C's keepers, trades places with whichever one touched him. Anyone who tags Middle C before he is supposed to do so has to pay a fine. (See Forfeits, p. 126.)

The players in the circle must use their daring and skill in coming close to B, C, and D but not close enough to be captured.

73

Attention to the area surrounding Middle C. Acquaintance with the upper and lower neighbors of Middle C.

BANNERS FLYING—PARADE OF THE TIME-VALUE REGIMENTS

Each time-value has its own regiment of toy soldiers; each regiment has its own flag bearer. The first in line carries a banner, which consists of its symbol on a cloth or large piece of paper taped to a yardstick. If the idea of toy soldiers is to be completely helpful we must imagine them as having many loose joints. The arms of the paraders must swing freely with no suggestion of stiffness. Both arms swing in the same direction like the two ropes of a swing.

Parade of the Quarter Notes

The children wear the large cutout quarter-note symbol or they may carry it as if it were a gun. The black elastic cord around the waist serves both to hold the quarter note, leaving their arms free to swing more easily, and also to demonstrate how a line cuts through the center of a note.

FIG. 42.   Parade of the Quarter Notes.

Practice swinging both arms back, then forward, back and forth. Both arms move together. Now take a step to each swing. Start with the arms swung back for the first step. Play incidental music for a Quarter Note March. Children say a one-

74

syllable abbreviation for quarter note: "Quart', quart', quart', quart'," for each measure of four quarter notes (four steps). Each syllable gets one swing and one step.

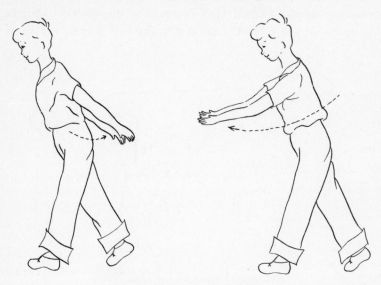

FIG. 43.   Step and swing.

Parade of the Half Notes

For the half notes, wear the half-note symbol (arm stuck through its hole) and take a step as both the arms swing back. Stay on that foot without another move other than swinging the arms forward for the second swing. As this is mastered, another coordination is added: say "Ha-alf" for the two swings and one step, beginning on the first swing back and holding the word for both swings. March to incidental music played in half-note units. Even if the leader has no piano, a great deal of benefit can be derived without accompanying music, because concentration and coordination are evoked. Children can sing the word "Ha-alf" drawn out for two beats up the scale or in any way they like. (Fig. 44.)

75

Parade of the Dotted Half Notes

This regiment, like its predecessors, wears its own uniform and is headed by a flag bearer whose banner carries the proud emblem of the Dotted Half Notes. For the dotted half-note uniform, attach a black paper dot to the half note by means of

FIG. 44. Parade of the Half Notes.

transparent tape, doubled to avoid a sticky surface. Let the children stick their arms through these notes "with holes in their heads." Through this kinesthetic experience they learn immediately to discriminate between quarter and half or dotted half notes.

A step is taken on the first of the three swings done with both arms together. Children notice that the step does not always start with a swing back, since, because of the odd number of beats we have "Down, up, down," for one step, and "Up, down, up" for the next step. Sing a single syllable like "Dah" holding it for the three swings "Da-a-a." Imagine the swinging arm is whispering "Dot-ted half," each swing being a syllable, while the step and the voice are holding the "Dah" for all three swings.

76

Parade of the Whole Notes

The whole note is easier and in some cases it is advisable to begin with it. The whole-note costumes should be worn as were the other symbols for each of the above. Step on the first swing back, and hold the foot in this position for the remaining three swings. The start on the backward swing is important as it leads to a feeling of "down, up, down, up" for later downbeat and up-beat consciousness.

On the Double (Eighth Notes Running)

The large cutout symbols for a pair of eighth notes must be large enough so that they may be worn as a collar.

Each child representing a pair of eighth notes swings both his arms in one direction as he takes two running steps. For example, as he swings his arms backward, he takes two running steps and as he swings his arms forward he takes the next two running steps.

FIG. 45.

Each quarter-note chord in incidental music (Figs. 45–49) should be divided into two eighth notes, to be played lightly. In other words each quarter note is played twice; thus instead of being quarter notes, the separate articulations represent eighth notes.

LEARNING GOAL: Concentration, coordination, and concepts.

FIG. 46.

In this activity which could be presented as a series of toy soldier parades where the marching mechanism seems to be winding down as the steps get spaced further apart, the child is able to feel the relationship of the rhythmic beats and the dif-

FIG. 47.

ferent time-values, thus developing rhythmic balance, coordination, and concentration as well as acquiring an understanding of the musical concepts involved.

FIG. 48.

Incidental Music for Time-Value Parades

These marches or processionals, may be used for time-value parades. They can be played in whatever units are required—all quarters, all halves, etc.

FIG. 49.   Processional in minor mode.

79

Use the second march (Fig. 46) for On the Double, playing each quarter divided into two eighths. In measures two and six, there already are two eighth notes on the fourth beat so it is not necessary to create eighth notes for this beat. Play the eighth notes that are written there.

BAR-LINES AND STAFF-LINES

Each staff-line is guarded by a Watchman. If there are ten or fewer players, not every line can be guarded, so each player must remember the unprotected lines. Two players are chosen to be the Bar-Lines, and they can run up or down the whole staff at the right edge opposite the clefs. They must avoid being tagged by the staff-line Watchmen. These stand near the clefs until a signal is given. They then run on their particular lines to try to tag the Bar-Lines, who keep running up and down the staff. A Watchman may tag a Bar-Line only when he is on the Watchman's particular line, and only on a signal from the referee.

LEARNING GOAL: Awareness of bar-lines; concentration on the staff-lines.

BEANBAG GAMES

Bag in the Basket

EQUIPMENT: Basket or bowl; black beanbag representing a note.

FORMATION: Players divide into bass-clef team and treble-clef team. Each chooses a Referee who stands beside the basket to pitch the bag back to the next player on his team. Both teams stand below the staff so that all will have a true image of the whole staff.

GAME: Referee puts the basket on the F line for the bass-clef team. From a position several feet below the staff, each member of the team in turn aims the beanbag at the basket. The Referee counts the points.

Every time someone lands the bag in the basket, the leader plays the tone F. Whenever the player lands the beanbag outside the basket, he takes his place wherever the bag landed. Group leader plays that tone and compares it with the F where the bag should have landed. The player must tell whether he landed above or below F.

When each member of the bass-clef team has had his turn, a basket is placed on the G line for the treble-clef team. The procedure is the same as that for the F line, with the players who miss the basket taking their places wherever the beanbag landed.

The distance from the basket may be reckoned by counting the number of lines of the staff away from the basket. By increasing the distance from the basket for both teams, they will be forced to think of imaginary lines below the staff, thus preparing for the later introduction of "leger-lines," imaginary lines above and below the staff that appear only in connection with a note in that location.

OPTIONAL: Indicate on a paper music staff the Notes that are standing. Play them and try to make a little tune out of them.

SCORING: Count one for landing on a first line (either staff) two for a second line, three for the third, four for the fourth, and five for the fifth line.

LEARNING GOAL: Strengthening the image of the Grand Staff, establishing the landmarks F and G; counting the lines and spaces to develop visual perception and a sense of space relationship; association of sound to staff; comparison of sounds to F and G; suggestion of leger-lines.

Center Base

FORMATION: Players stand on the staff or around it in a circle, but each must take his place on a definite line or space. The

Center player stands on any line of the staff he may choose. For instance, he might choose the G line from which to make his first throw of the beanbag to a player in the circle.

GAME: As soon as he has thrown the bag, Center breaks through the circle and runs around the outside to appropriate the spot vacated by the catcher. The circle player is required to return the beanbag to the line chosen by Center as his base, and then follow Center's exact trail on his way "home" to resume his place in the circle. In this game a great deal may depend on Center's alertness in recognizing the line or space where the circle player stood. For the circle player, speedy and accurate perception of Center's trail is a vital necessity.

If the circle player succeeds in beating Center back into his old place in the circle and staff, he is promoted to Center. Otherwise he steps back into the circle and Center retains his supremacy.

Dodge Note

FORMATION: Players are divided into two teams; Lines and Notes. Lines stand on lines inside the staff; Notes surround the staff.

GAME: At a signal, Notes throw paper notes or beanbags toward the lines of the staff. If any line is hit, the player representing that line must leave the staff and join the Notes. The object is to see who can stay in the staff longest without having his line hit. As soon as all Lines are out, sides change and the game continues.

If notes of different values are used for throwing, the player whose line has been hit will be slapped on the back once for a quarter note, twice for a half note, three times for a dotted half, and four for a whole note. Give each note thrower a set of notes in these different time-values. The player who threw the note successfully does the back slapping.

82

Leader and Group

FORMATION: Players stand in a diagonal row up the staff, G, A, B, etc. They face the top line of the staff. The Leader stands at an equal distance from each of the players as she throws a beanbag to each in turn. As each player catches the beanbag, he must sing his alphabet name and toss the bag back to the Leader.

Ideally, the Leader should be one of the children and the group leader should be able to sound the pitch for each child's note. If this is not possible out-of-doors, an Autoharp, a pitch pipe, or a toy xylophone can be used, and the notes on the staff can be limited to those represented on the instrument.

This would necessitate a smaller group of players, and the action would be confined to the treble staff. The specially prepared Autoharp described on page 50 would furnish the sounds for *all* the lines and spaces on the playing field.

Even without an instrument the group can begin on Middle C and sing the alphabet names of the C major scale. These are the same tones as for do-re-mi, but the alphabet letters C, D, E, F, G, A, B, and C are substituted. With a piano or full-range instrument, of course there is no problem.

GAME: Each player is required to catch the beanbag when it is tossed to him and to sing his musical name correctly. If he fails, he goes to the foot of the staff or the lowest note that is being used. If the Leader fails to catch the bag as it is thrown back to her, she becomes the lowest Note on the staff. The one who was top Note becomes Leader.

Staff Board Game

EQUIPMENT: A board about 4′ × 3′; small black beanbags. A large board on which a music staff is painted is slanted against anything that will hold it up at any angle. The lines of the staff must be sufficiently far apart to allow a hole in each space large enough to permit a small beanbag to pass through. The holes

83

can be cut in a diagonal slant up the board. Besides the holes in the spaces within the bass and treble staves, there would be two holes, one below Middle C and one above.

The scoring system would be one point for a throw either through the first space in the bass clef (the space above the bottom line), or through the space above the bottom line of

Fig. 50. The black circles represent the holes; the numbers need not appear on the staff board. They appear in the drawing to indicate the scoring. Allow ten points for each throw in the BCD Land.

the treble clef; two points for a second space, three for a third space, etc.; ten points would be scored for landing in the space above or below Middle C.

Target Note

A note is placed on the bottom line of the playing field and each player has a chance to hit it. If he does so, the note is moved to the next higher line. The target is moved progressively higher each time. The player must remember at what line he missed, and the line should be marked with his initials on a music staff kept by the leader as a scoreboard and reminder. The first to hit the note on all lines wins.

To prolong the game, the target note may be placed on the spaces as well as the lines.

Where Was I? (for five and six-year-olds in a small room)

The children stand below the staff. The Leader stands on a specific line or space, throws the beanbag to a child, then steps off the staff. The child who caught the beanbag must return it to the exact spot from which it was thrown. If he is correct, he becomes the Leader, and he may choose his own line or space from which to throw the beanbag.

As soon as he throws the beanbag, he jumps off the staff, crying, "Where was I?"

Zigzag Note in C Major

FORMATION: One row of players stands on spaces; another row stands facing them but these stand on lines. The first player stands on the second space in the bass clef. The first player in the row facing him will be on the third line D. In the first row which will be on the left of the staff, there will be a player on space C, space E, and continuing up the staff if there are no more than eight players. If there are more, the spaces will be filled up to the third space C in the treble clef.

FIG. 51. Notes represent players: one row on spaces, another on lines, all in C major. Beanbag is thrown from space to line to next space, etc.

85

Opposite this row are the players on lines. Starting with the third bass line D, all the lines are filled up to the third treble line B if there are enough players. If only eight, begin the line-row on Middle C. (See Fig. 52.)

GAME: The players sing their names on pitch as they throw the bag from space to line and back to space across the two rows. For ease in singing and in getting some help from a pitch pipe, the formation could begin with Middle C and go up one octave (i.e., just to the C above, third space.) Here, the lines would be on the left and the spaces in the row on the right.

FIG. 52.

LEARNING GOAL (for all beanbag games): Strengthening the staff image; developing visual perception and a sense of space relationship; discriminating between lines and spaces; establishing landmarks; associating sounds with locations on the staff.

BIG NOTE CUTOUT

EQUIPMENT: Construction paper, scissors, transparent tape.

Step 1. Cut out a large quarter note. Act out its time-value as in Banners Flying. Each child may place his quarter note on a line or space specified by the leader or another child of his own choosing.

Step 2. Pick up the same quarter notes and cut a hole in the center of the note-head. This is easily done by folding the note-head before cutting. The hole converts the quarter into a half note. Act out its time-value and engage in other activities suggested by the leader. Sing "Ha-alf" as one continuous sound while giving two swings.

Step 3. Cut out a large dot and attach it to the half note with a small piece of transparent tape. Put another piece of tape over the sticky side of the first to achieve a smooth surface. Act out the time-value of the dotted half note. Sing "Do-o-ot" for one dotted half note, "te-e-ed" for the next dotted half note, "ha-a-alf" for a third, and "no-o-ote" for the last, giving three swings to each of these four dotted half notes.

Step 4. This is the unkindest cut of all! Clip off the stem and the beautifully attached dot. You now have a whole note, to which you sing "Who-o-o-ole" as you give four swings. Act out its duration with marching and swinging and wear it as a crown for your fine work.

LEARNING GOAL: Alternation of quiet occupation with lively physical movement; time-value concepts.

BLACK AND WHITE COIN TOSS

EQUIPMENT: A coin or checker, one side covered with black tape, the other with white. (Any other way of obtaining the same effect is just as good.)

FORMATION: One group is called Black Lines and the other White Spaces. They stand between the two staves with the Referee who tosses the coin. He catches it in his hand and calls "Black" or "White" depending on the result of the throw.

The side named must run to take places. If the black side turned up, Blacks would take places on lines; if white showed up, Whites would take places on different spaces. (No two players can be on the same line or space.) The opposing side tries to tag the others before they settle into their newly-found "homes." Losers must change sides in the next game.

LEARNING GOAL: A helpful transition to the concept of black lines, of particular use for playgrounds where the staff is drawn in yellow. Discrimination between lines and spaces.

BLACKBERRY HILL

EQUIPMENT: First the children cut little notes out of black paper. The quarter note will be the berry on a stem. The "berries" are placed in the spaces between the paths, which are the lines. (Include the spaces above and below the magic Middle C line.)

GAME: The leader will ask the children to line up behind her on the left side of the staff near the clefs. She will explain that they are going for a hike up Blackberry Hill. No one is to pick any berries until they have all reached the top of the hill which is the staff itself. The paths are narrow so they must put one foot in front of the other carefully in order not to get scratched by the bushes. Anyone getting off the path must cry, "Ouch."

Then the leader starts off on a path from the left to the right of the staff, going all the way around to start from the left again on the next path. On each trip the children will notice where the most berries grow.

When the whole group reaches the top of the hill, everyone will scatter to pick as many berries as he can, but each picker must stand on only one path to do so.

Each path will be numbered, beginning with the bottom line as Path Number One. After the fifth line or path, the Middle C line is not to be counted although the group will walk along it, being careful not to brush against berry bushes on either side of it. The path on the next line above is Path Number One again in the treble (G) clef.

When the leader has coached the children in the manner of taking this hike, she may go to the piano and play a rhythmic series of tones corresponding to whatever lines they are on. They feel that the paths are really going uphill, as the tones for each path become higher and higher.

These words might be intoned for each path:

> Blackberry picking on Blackberry Hill
> Path Number _____, our baskets will fill.

On the Middle C line they simply chant, "Path Middle C our baskets will fill."

Even though their voices cannot sing as low as the low tones for the bass lines, it is the awareness of the low tones that counts here. As long as they listen carefully and make an effort to chant the words to the pitch, that is all that is necessary. In the treble, of course, they will be able to sing the verse on pitch.

LEARNING GOAL: Association of pitch with the lines. Noticing the relationships of the lines through counting their number.

BLINDMAN'S BUFF

High or Low

EQUIPMENT: Cutout notes, handkerchief for a blindfold.

GAME: One child is blindfolded and stands in the center of a circle of children who stand on the lines of the staff. They hold their cutout notes against themselves in such a way as to suggest their staff location. Imagining the bottom line of either staff as their shoes, the middle line on either staff as their belts, and the top line of the bass or treble as a hat, they approximate the other two lines of the staff on themselves in relationship to the bottom, middle, and top lines.

Blindman turns around as the others sing:

> I'm very, very high.
> I'm very, very low.

Sometimes high and sometimes low
Guess what I am now.

(The line with the word "high" should be sung at a high pitch
and the line with the word "low" at a low pitch.)

The Blindman touches a player and tries to guess what line
his note is on by feeling. Therefore it is important that each
child hold his note against himself to correspond as accurately
as possible with its location on the staff. The leader can help
the Blindman by playing the note he is trying to identify, and
the children can hum the tone each time he makes a guess. If he
guesses correctly, he trades places with the circle child.

Variation

If notes of different time-values are used, Blindman must also
guess what kind of note the child is holding—quarter, half,
dotted half, or whole note, using the sound and shape as clues.

LEARNING GOAL: Association of pitch with the lines of the staff;
a personal involvement through the transfer of the space relationships on the staff to their own bodies.

Note Exchange

GAME: Middle C is blindfolded and stands on a black strip
that indicates his special little line. The other players can draw
lots to decide which line or space they are to stand on. The lots
to be drawn will be small pieces of regular music paper with
both staves present and one note marked on it. On the line or
space that each child occupies, mark a particular spot with chalk
or decide that each Note will stand as close to the clefs as
possible.

The object of the game is for two Notes to trade places as
noiselessly as possible and to escape being caught by Middle C.
It is Middle C who calls out two letters, such as F and A. These
two are the ones to trade places. Neither may move more than

FIG. 53.   High or low (Blindman's Buff).

one step to the right or left from where he stands on his line or space. If Middle C can capture one of the traders, he and his captive trade places, Middle C becoming a Note on the line or space of the captured Note and the captive becoming Middle C. Middle C can also specify a Note in a particular clef—"Treble G and Bass F trade places."

LEARNING GOAL: Attention to the special line for Middle C and a rapid response to the names of the lines and spaces.

Swinging Stick

EQUIPMENT: Yardstick or cane.

GAME: Players form a circle. As they move around they step only on lines. Center player holding a cane is blindfolded and he stands on a black line put down at Middle C, or he stands at F in the bass or G in the treble. He may choose his position before the game starts. Players move around until Blindman taps his cane. He may tap once, twice, three, or four times. When he finishes tapping, he points his stick at one of the circle players. The child at whom he points takes the end of the stick extended toward him.

"Make a sound like a half note" says Blindman if he has tapped his cane twice. If he has tapped once he asks for the sound of a quarter; if three times, for a dotted half, and if four times, for a whole note.

The circle child holding the end of the cane swings it twice as he sings, "La-ah," thinking two syllables but singing one continuous sound. For a quarter, the child swings once and sings "Lah." For a dotted half, he swings the stick three times, singing "Lah-ah-ah," and for four swings for the whole note, he sings "Lah-ah-ah-ah." (See Syllables and Swings, p. 15.)

Blindman must guess the line occupied by the singing child, who may give Blindman a hint by tapping the number of his line on the Blindman's cane. Blindman still has to guess the

92

name of the line and its clef. (For three taps, the Blindman might venture this guess, "Third line in the bass, D.") If the guess is correct, the two trade places. (Younger groups need only number the line, not name it.)

LEARNING GOAL: Physical and vocal interpretations of time-values.

CANDY CAROLS

EQUIPMENT: A Grand Staff painted with a felt nib pen, on a yard length of white oilcloth or drawer-lining paper. Some Life-savers, gumdrops, colored straws cut into short lengths; long, thin candy sticks, or chocolate-flavored straws.

ACTIVITY: If it happens to be holiday time, it is fun to copy the notes of any familiar Christmas carol, using the Lifesavers for half notes or whole notes, the straws for stems where needed. The quarters and eighths can be made out of gumdrops, with the straws or long, narrow candies serving as stems and bars.

Variation

Equipment same as above except each child gets a piece of lining paper on which he draws his own Grand Staff. He is given some of the candy and straws with which he "writes" a few measures of a specified tune, either one that has been done by the whole group on the oilcloth or one that the leader specifies and presents in whatever form she chooses. Dictation is very interesting to try. Those who get it right, eat their candy.

LEARNING GOAL: In addition to the combined sensory channels of sight, hearing, and touch, the senses of taste and of smell enter into the learning experience as the fragrant and mouth-watering candies make "writing" notes and taking musical dicta-tion a delightful and delicious demonstration.

CHANGE BASES

FORMATION: The leader assigns Notes to various lines and spaces arranged in a circle about the staff, marking their positions on a slate or large sheet of paper with a staff on it.

One member of the group will take his place in the center on Middle C. He will act as the Caller. When bases are changed, the players must run around the outside of the staff. Crossing through the center is not allowed.

GAME: Middle C repeats this verse several times:

> Notes on a space,
> Notes on a line!
> Change your base
> When I give the sign!

He may say this over and over again but no one is to move. Whenever he decides to, he may call "Change!" and everyone is to change places. Middle C tries to get on one of the other bases. If he is successful, the player left out becomes Middle C. Since the word "Change" is the first word in the third line of the verse, the players never know whether he is really going to end right on that word or go on.

At the end of the game, forfeits are exacted for changing before the signal and for being caught off base. It is important for each player to remember the line on which he was caught away from home, for he will be charged in proportion to its location. If he was on the first line, it will cost him one point; the second, two points, etc. The scoring is similar for spaces, beginning with the loss of one point for the first space, and so on progressively.

Initials can be marked on the music-staff scoreboard as a help in settling the score.

LEARNING GOAL: Concentration on the staff.

CHASING TIME-VALUES I

EQUIPMENT: Cutout notes of different time-values, quarters, half notes, dotted half notes, and whole notes (eighths optional) are put into a hat or box, and the children draw to see what time-value they will represent. If cutout notes are not available, the notes may be written on slips of paper, but there must be at least two of each time-value. Each child keeps his paper or cutout which in this case must be very small.

GAME: Two children draw for one of the two clefs instead of notes. If one draws the bass, the other will be the treble. Then the Clefs take their stand on their symbols on the playing field. The Clefs are not to know which children represent which notes. They close their eyes and call, "Whole, Half," etc. Each chooses an equal number of players for his side, but there must be at least one of each time-value represented on each team. Bass Clef stations his players on his bottom line and Treble Clef on his top line.

Bass calls first, "Whole notes exchange places." Treble tries to tag one of the Notes while they are in the act of exchanging places. Whenever he catches a Note, he slaps him lightly on the back the number of beats represented by each Note. (See Feeling the Beat, p. 122.) The next turn, Treble does the calling and Bass tries to catch one of his Notes. The caller may not move from his place.

Each Clef must play the time-values he has caught. The Clef with the highest number of points represented by the collected beats of the different Notes, wins.

CHASING TIME-VALUES II

The players draw slips of paper from a box or bag. These slips bear the sign of a quarter note, a half note, a dotted half note, a whole note, or an eighth note. On further acquaintance with the game, rest symbols may also be used. (See p. 186.)

One child is appointed Treble Clef. He stands on his symbol on the playing field. All the others stand huddled together on the top line of the treble clef as far from Clef himself as possible. If there are more children than can get on one line, they stand in a tight group as close to the top line as possible.

Suddenly Treble or G Clef calls the name of a time-value—"Quarter!" for instance. All the children who represent quarter notes—and there may be a number in each category—run to the F line in the bass with Treble Clef in pursuit, trying to tag them before they reach the safety of the bass line. In this game the Treble Clef does not know in advance which children represent the time-value that he has chosen.

The next round of the game is played from the bass clef with one child appointed to be the Bass or F Clef and to stand on his symbol until it is time to chase the time-values he has called. In this round, the Notes draw for their time-values all over again, stand on the lowest far corner of the bass clef, and those who are called run toward the G line in the treble when Bass Clef calls out their names.

LEARNING GOAL: Recognition of different time-values.

CONDUCTING FOR BEGINNERS

Cheer Leaders (3/4 time)

Each child will be an imaginary cheer leader in front of an imaginary audience.

STAGE I: the cheer

> Down—right—up!
> Down—right—up!
> One—two—three!
> One—two—three!
> TRI—AN—GLE!
> TRI—AN—GLE!

96

YAY—AY—AY!!!
YAY—AY—AY!!! (one long YAAAY)

Now for the motions to accompany this cheer.

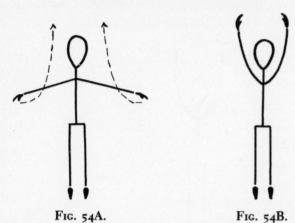

FIG. 54A.   FIG. 54B.

Giving the cue to the audience: This is the "Are you ready?":
Bring the audience to its feet with a swinging motion of both
arms from out at your sides to above your head, as you rise
on tiptoes. (See Figs. 54A and 54B.)

Calisthenics

The calisthenics to accompany the above cheer are as follows:
Down (on the first beat), squat, bringing both arms to the

FIG. 54C.   FIG. 54D.

97

floor to the left of the body. Bend slightly to the left at the waist and touch fingertips to floor. (Figs. 54C.)

Right (on the second beat), remaining in same position, sweep arms to the right, across but above the floor and touch fingertips to the right of the body. (Fig. 54D.)

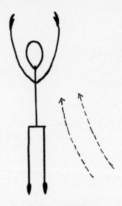

Fig. 54E.

Up (third beat which is the upbeat), spring back to upright position same as for the cue, "Are you ready?"—up on toes, arms above head. Although it is the same position as the "Are you ready?" it represents in this case the third beat or upbeat in a 3/4 time measure. Repeat seven more times, the equivalent of eight measures or length of the cheer. (Fig. 54E.)

STAGE II: (position for "Are you ready?")

Left—right—up!
Left—right—up!
One—two—three!
One—two—three!
TRI—AN—GLE!
TRI—AN—GLE!
YAY—AY—AY!!!
YAY—AY—AY!!!

98

The last "YAAAY" should be prolonged as before, and followed by a free jump in the air.

Calisthenics

Take pencil or ruler in right hand, holding it at one end (thumb on underside of pencil and other fingers on top side). The motions are essentially the same as in Stage I except that here one arm remains at the side quietly while only the right arm swings.

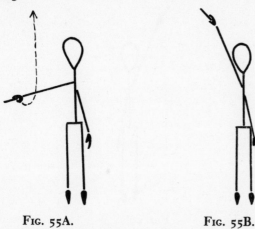

FIG. 55A.   FIG. 55B.

Rise to tiptoes with pencil above center of head as far as you can reach. This is the "Are you ready?" or cue. (Figs. 55A and 55B.)

Left (first or downbeat), squat, bending slightly to the left at

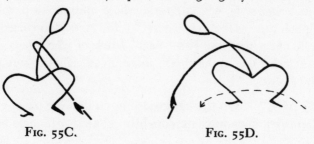

FIG. 55C.   FIG. 55D.

the waist and touching tip of pencil to the floor, far left of the body. (Fig. 55C.)

Right (second beat), remaining in squatting position, carry right arm in wide arc across the floor or just sweep pencil across the floor, landing tip at the far right of body, bending to the right at waist. (Fig. 55D.)

Up (third beat, also called upbeat), spring back to same posision as in the cue, "Are you ready?" except that this swinging

FIG. 55E.

up to rise on toes and to swing the pencil far above the head is the third beat or upbeat in a 3/4 time measure. (Fig. 55E.)

These movements should accompany the words of the cheer. The "YAAAY!!!" (or Yay-ay-ay!), with a leap in the air in typical cheer-leader style, will last for a whole measure so it will take as much time as the "TRI-AN-GLE" or the "ONE-TWO-THREE!" The whole cheer with the two "Yays" (each of which last as long as any other line in the cheer) make up an eight-measure phrase in 3/4 time.

STAGE III: On the blackboard or on drawing paper clipped to an easel, draw in chalk (brightly colored) a triangle figure—

all sides even. Without squatting or bending or touching the floor, use the essential motions of down—right—up as in the gymnastics. Keep retracing the figure as you continue saying the words of the cheer.

In the word "triangle," each syllable will represent its own side of the triangle drawing. The word "yay" (or really "yay-ay-ay") prolonged for three beats represents the complete triangle.

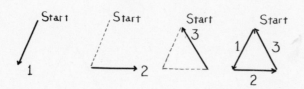

FIG. 56.   Triangular conducting pattern in 3/4 time.

Number the sides: (1) at the bottom of the left side, since this is where the first beat actually falls, then (2) at the right corner of the bottom side, since the crayon or chalk reaches here directly on the second beat and (3) near the top of the right side. Place this (3) slightly below the top to avoid confusion with the starting point.

CONDUCTING DESIGN (3/4 time—Triangle Tracing)

Make a triangle by placing three different colored pipe cleaners on paper, one for each side of a triangle. Tape them down where the tips meet at the corners.

As you run your fingers along each fuzzy side, the pleasurable tactile sensation will reinforce the visual impression.

Small bells on a string (such as are often used to sew on costumes) may be taped to the corners. The tinkle of the bells adds another pleasant sensory element. (See Fig. 57.)

101

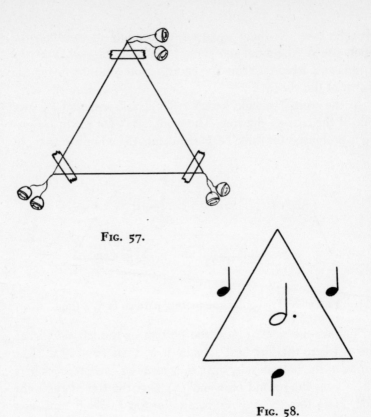

Fig. 57.

Fig. 58.

Paste a cutout quarter note at the outside of each side of the triangle and a dotted half note within the triangle. (Fig. 58.)

Music for Conducting

For a list of suitable songs and other music for this elementary conducting see Appendix. The following song, "My Name Is Susie," presents the minimum of difficulty since it consists of quarter and dotted half notes exclusively.

Sing this little song:

My name is Susie and I like to play (pla-a-ay)
What did you think I was going to say? (sa-a-ay)

FIG. 59. "My Name Is Susie."

The name must always have two syllables so if you have a John in the group he would have to sing, "Johnnie." In addition to choosing a nickname for himself, each child may choose a different word of *one* syllable for the last word in the first line, as a substitute for the word "play." One might substitute the word "sleep" or "run" or "eat," etc. This word must be held for three counts (three sides of the triangle). The word "say" at the end of the song also gets a whole triangle or three beats. (Each side represents one beat.) All the other syllables get one side apiece, as they appear in the song as quarter notes. The finger retraces the triangular "conducting design" for the duration of the whole song.

LEARNING GOAL: Importance of holding a dotted half note for three beats. Understanding of 3/4 time through a graphic presentation of an abstract idea. Using the whole body to learn the rudimentary baton technique for conducting 3/4 time. Greater appreciation of the orchestra or band leader.

Cheer Leaders (4/4 time)

STAGE I: the cheer

> Down—left—right—up!
> Down—left—right—up!
> Who—are—we—for?
> We're—for—four-four!
> Down—left—right—up!
> Down—left—right—up!
> YA-YA-AY-AY!!!!
> YA-AY-AY-AY!!!!

Calisthenics

The calisthenics to accompany the above cheer are as follows: "Take a deep breath, everybody. Up on your toes, arms out at the sides, then swing your arms up above your head. "Are you ready?" This is the cue. (Figs. 60A and B.)

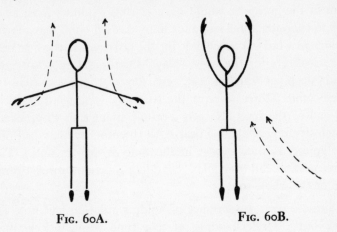

FIG. 60A.   FIG. 60B.

On the downbeat (count one, squat, bringing both hands down to the ground in front of you, fingertips touching the floor. (Fig. 60C.)

FIG. 60C.

On the word "left" (second beat), bend to the left from the waist, still remaining in the squatting position, swinging both arms to the left in an arc and letting fingertips touch the floor. (Fig. 60D.)

On the word "right" (third beat), bend to the right, swinging both arms to the right in a wide arc, touching fingertips to the floor. (Fig. 60E.)

FIG. 60E.

On the word "up" (fourth beat and also upbeat), spring back to position taken in giving the cue, standing on tiptoe,

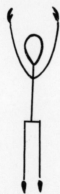

FIG. 60F.

holding both arms above the head. This routine accompanying the cheer-leading words should be performed to a slow, march-like piece in 4/4 time. (See p. 79.)

LEARNING GOAL: Acquiring through the large physical movements the basis for the baton movements necessary to conduct music in 4/4 time. Getting the downbeat concept on the first beat of the measure and the upbeat concept for the last beat of the measure.

STAGE II: Repeat this routine, holding a pencil in the right hand. This time leave the left arm quietly at the side and execute all the arm-swinging motions used before with the right arm only.

Calisthenics

The cue or "Get Ready": Rise on toes, swing the pencil tip to a foot or so above the center of your head. Now!

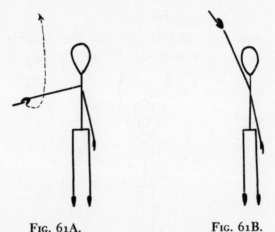

FIG. 61A.   FIG. 61B.

Down (first beat), squat, pencil tip touching floor in center front of body. (Fig. 61C.)

106

Fig. 61C.

Left (second beat), bend at waist to left, swing arm in wide arc, landing pencil tip on floor as far left of the body as possible. (Fig. 61D.)

Fig. 61D.

Right (third beat), bend to right at waist, swinging arm in wide arc to right, touching pencil tip to floor as far right of body as possible. (Fig. 61E.)

Fig. 61E.

Up (fourth beat), rise, stretch up on toes, pencil back to starting position above the head. (Fig. 61F.)

107

FIG. 61F.

STAGE III: Go to the blackboard (or to a large poster-board held vertically in front of you) and go through the same basic movements with a piece of chalk or crayon, marking the paper or board as you do so—the "down" with a

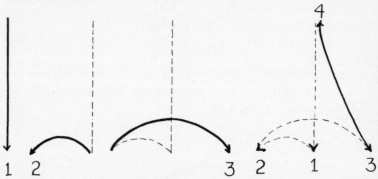

FIG. 62.   4/4 time conducting designs.

straight vertical line, "left" with an arc to the left, and "right" with an arc to the right. Then make a swinging curve up to meet the beginning of the downbeat line. The only movement that is not represented by a chalk mark is the preliminary cue which is a swing similar to the upbeat swing on the fourth count.

Conducting Design—(4/4 time)—"Butterflies and Bows"

Play a record of "Stars and Stripes," or sing "Yankee Doodle," "Mary Had a Little Lamb," or any other 4/4 tune (see list in Appendix p. 241) while drawing and tracing this butterfly or bow-tie figure over and over. Each completed figure represents a measure in 4/4 time. Note that the *downbeat is the only vertical straight line.*

Tape colored pipe cleaners over this figure drawn on paper. Use a different color for each representation of a beat. Downbeat (the vertical straight line) might be green, arc to the left

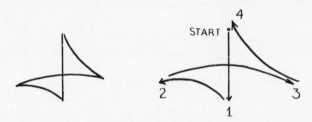

Fig. 63. Butterflies and bows. The upswing on "4" is also the movement for the cue, "Are you ready?"

might be red; arc to the right, blue; and upbeat, orange. For an intense tactile sensation, move right index finger on the fuzzy surface, following the direction of the arrows in the diagram.

Next time you have an opportunity to hear a symphony concert you will find yourself watching the conductor with new understanding. This is only the faintest glimmer of all the intricate time-beating that he must do and that is only the smallest part of his task.

Conducting Two Christmas Carols*

"WE THREE KINGS OF ORIENT ARE":   This is an illustration of
3/4 conducting (triangle tracing).

The first word "We" gets two sides of the triangle because it
is worth two beats. The word "three" coincidentally gets the
third side of the triangle and thus ends one measure of the
song.

"Kings" gets two sides traced and "of" gets the third side.
Each syllable of "O-ri-ent" gets a side to itself, the last word
"are" is held while all three sides are traced.

FIG. 64.   "We Three Kings of Orient Are."

Notice that the words that get two sides equal a half note;
words or even separate syllables that get only one side equal a
quarter note; the word that lasts a whole measure is a dotted
half note.

"GOOD KING WENCESLAS" (4/4 conducting):   This sturdy old
carol furnishes an excellent opportunity for elementary conducting in 4/4 time, since it is composed entirely of quarter and
half notes. Allow one sweeping stroke for each quarter, two
sweeping strokes for each half note. Use the "butterfly" 4/4
time conducting design. A whole note at the very end of the
song calls for the tracing of the entire "butterfly."

---

* These carols have been successfully presented as pantomimes. Having a
group of children conduct the singing adds to the musical interest.

FIG. 65. "Good King Wenceslas."

COUNTING MEASURES I

EQUIPMENT: Conducting designs from CHEER LEADERS, pp. 102, 109 for 3/4 and 4/4.

The design should have long pipe cleaners taped on the top of the drawing. These give a tactile sensation as the finger moves along each side of the triangle or the sweeping curves of the "butterfly." Music in the appropriate time signature should accompany this activity. (See p. 238.)

GAME: One child is the Referee. He decides how many measures in a particular time signature are to be counted: eight, ten, twelve. The Referee also decides on a goal line for each round of the game. The others—the Measure-Counters—stand below the staff (below the bottom G line of the bass) and go through these measures by tracing and retracing the conducting design for the time signature chosen by the Referee.

At the end of the exact number of measures, the players race to the designated line in the treble staff. First one to touch the line and return home wins and becomes Referee.

Anyone "jumping the gun," that is, not finishing the full number of measures, must pay a forfeit. He must count one measure on the first line, two on the second, three on the third, etc. on one or both staves, according to the Referee's decision.

Whatever variations are added, the important element to retain is the counting of measures by the completion of each form.

COUNTING MEASURES II

The Referee orders the players to be Cheer Leaders again and leap into the air with a loud Yay! but not until a secret signal has been given. Instead of telling them when to jump and cheer, he merely tells them the number of measures in a certain time signature to wait before jumping.

He gives the upbeat or preparation by swinging both arms from out at his sides to above his head, and demonstrates one full measure in either the "left, right, up" of the 3/4 or the "down, left, right, up" of the 4/4. Then he gives the upbeat or cue to start and they follow. They go on for the number of measures he has specified while he folds his arms and waits.

As they silently go through the cheer-leading routine, they count only the downbeat represented by the strong downward motion which takes place on the "one" of each measure. This is the "left" on the "left, right, up" of the three-four time and the "down" of the "down, left, right, up" of the four-four time.

At the end of the designated number of measures, the Cheer Leaders leap into the air and cry "Yay"! Anyone jumping up to give the cheer before the appointed time must pay a forfeit.

COUNTING ON THE FINGERS

Select a song in 4/4 or 3/4 that starts on the count of "one" (the downbeat) in the first measure. Preferably it should have mostly quarter and half notes in it. See Appendix for a listing of songs suitable for this purpose. Songs in 2/4 are not recommended as a beginning even though the conducting of each measure is a simple "down, up," because the measures pass by too quickly to allow sufficient time for the beginner to dwell on each measure as a unit and to make the responses necessary to counting in terms of measures, in addition to counting each beat within the measure.

Divide the players into Singers, Conductors, and Measure Counters. While one group sings, the second group goes through the conducting motions appropriate to the time signature chosen. The third group must count the beats in each measure silently and bend a finger on the "one" of each measure. The leader may interrupt at any time and ask, "How many measures have been sung?" The Measure-Counters must hold up the last finger they have bent; this should help give the answer because each finger represents a different number.

Beginning with the left hand, thumb stands for first measure, index for second measure, middle for the third measure, ring finger for fourth, smallest finger for fifth. The sixth measure will be the thumb on the right hand, seventh will be right index, eighth the right middle finger, etc. After finishing the tenth measure with the smallest finger on the right hand, the eleventh measure would go back to the left hand thumb and continue in the same manner.

Each Measure Counter should be inwardly saying, "One, two, three, four" (provided the song is in 4/4) and bending a finger on each "one." The trick is to gain enough control to substitute an ordinal number for each "one." First, two, three, four—

Second, two, three, four—Third, two, three, four—Fourth, two, three, four—.

The story is told of a tympani player who quietly sneaked out while a symphony concert was going on. Seated in the tavern near Carnegie Hall, he could be heard muttering to himself between sips of beer, "Seventy-five, two, three, four—Seventy-six, two, three, four, etc."

He had a hundred measures of rest before his next entrance and it was a very long, slow movement.

COVER THE SPACES

Middle C sits on a black stick or paper strip off the staff but between the treble and bass staves. Imagine that the Middle C line extends to the left and right of the staff. The other children sit or stand in the spaces.

Player in the lowest space issues the command, "Move up!" whereupon each player must rise and move into the next higher space. Top space-sitter will be pushed off the staff proper. It is now a question of who can get to the vacated bottom space first. Middle C and the player originally on top space race each other to get into it. (See Fig. 66.)

Middle C must first run along the imaginary Middle C line into the center of the staff and from there run for the bottom space. Without this requirement, he would always have the advantage over the occupant of the top space who would have farther to run. Loser becomes Middle C and must sit on his black strip.

This game can be played on lines as well. The players may be directed by the occupant of the highest position on the staff to move down. In this case, Middle C and bottom player race for the top line or space. Middle C must again come into the staff first on his own line before heading for the top goal.

LEARNING GOAL: Reading readiness.

FIG. 66.   Cover the spaces.

CROSSING THE ROAD

GAME: The players stand on the F line. The first player at the left decides by what route he will get to the G line in the treble. He may step on the next space G (above the F line), then jump to Middle C and from there jump to treble line G.

Each player is allowed four moves to get to G, but no two players may use the same moves. (Count starting line and finish line as two moves.) A corresponding sound for each move should be played on an instrument.

At first, the Referee could decide that the number of moves be limited to three. This would make it easier for the players to remember the moves already made. The Referee should have a music notebook or blackboard on which he can record the moves by putting a mark or a notehead on the lines and spaces used by each player. Use a measure for each player, put his name above the Grand Staff and a double bar at the end of the measure to separate it from the "score" for the next player.

As the players gain more security in remembering moves, the Referee should increase the moves to four and finally five.

LEARNING GOAL: Memory training; awareness of musical patterns; adjustment of visual focus from playing field to music tablet or blackboard staff.

DOTTED HALF NOTE CHASE
(Inspired by folk game Hound and Hare)

FORMATION: Groups of three children form a triangle by stretching their arms out to the side and resting their hands on each others' shoulders. A larger triangle can be made if they stretch out their arms and merely touch fingertips, but although this is better physical exercise, it is a more tiring position to maintain. Each triangle represents a measure in 3/4 time. A child wearing a dotted half note symbol stands in the center of

116

each of these triangles. Two children stay outside. One is a Dotted Half Note without a home (a measure), and the other is the Piano Player.

GAME: At a signal from the Leader, Player chases the extra Dotted Half Note, who runs in under the arms of the players forming a triangle. No measure in 3/4 time may contain more than one Dotted Half Note, so as soon as the extra Note enters a measure, the old occupant must run out and be chased by Player.

Whenever the Player catches a homeless Note, Player chooses a side of a triangle, (any triangle), to become the extra Dotted Half and the Dotted Half who is caught becomes the next Player.

LEARNING GOAL: Time-value concept.

DREAMING CLEF

EQUIPMENT: Cutout note symbols or paper bags with different time-values drawn on them. These paper bags will be worn by the captured Notes.

FORMATION: One child takes the part of either Treble Clef or Bass Clef. If the game is to begin with Bass Clef, the group forms around Clef who crouches on his sign. The group, who have appointed one member to be Leader of the Notes, move in a circle around Clef.

GAME: Crouching Clef, eyes closed, says, "I'm dreaming of some nice juicy Notes, one for the second space (C), one for the fifth line (A), etc. He may name as many places as he likes; meanwhile the circle continues to move around him. As soon as he mentions the fourth line (F), which is the special line designated by the Bass or F Clef, the circle stops moving.

Leader of the Notes says, "What kind of note do wou want?"

117

Clef may say, "A Whole Note."

Leader says, "Where will you put him?"

Clef tells on which line or space of his clef he will place his captive Note. Then he rises, uncovers his face, and chases the Notes who run away from him.

Anyone he catches, he slaps lightly according to the time-value that he announced to the Leader. Since in this example he said "Whole Note," Clef brings his hand down lightly on the Note's back or hand, and leaves it down as he swings from side to side four times: left, right, left, right. (See "Feeling the Beat" p. 122.)

Clef now puts either a cutout symbol or a note hat (decorated with a whole note) on his captive and leads him to a special place on Clef's own staff.

Leader of the Notes now becomes the new Clef, (this time Treble Clef). He too sits crouched, face covered, in the center of the treble staff while the others, having appointed a Leader of the Notes, circle around him.

Clef muses, "I'm dreaming about some nice, juicy Notes, one for the third line B, one for the first space F (younger groups, who do not know the alphabet names, are required only to name the number of line or space.) As soon as he mentions, "Second line G" which is the line specially designated by G Clef (other name for Treble Clef), the circling stops and Leader of Notes asks the same questions as before.

As soon as Clef answers, he chases the Notes and the same slapping of the time-value takes place when he has made his catch. Then he puts the note symbol on his captive and leads him to a line or space in the treble clef.

The leader should decide whether the captured Notes should remain on the places in the staff to which Clef has led them. In case they are to remain, no other Note may be put on that line and Clef may not mention that line or space when he is dreaming of the Notes he wants to catch.

The game continues with constant alternation of clef.

LEARNING GOAL: Reading readiness and time-value concept.

DROP THE NOTE

FORMATION: All players except one form a circle on the musical playing field, each standing on a specific line of the staff even though he has joined hands with his neighbors on the right and left to form a part of the circle.

GAME: The player who is IT carries a small note cut out of rubber. He runs around the outside of the circle to choose a player behind whom he will drop the note. None of the other players are allowed to turn their heads to watch him. IT will make every effort to deceive the others by pretending to drop the note at various times.

As soon as a player discovers the note actually placed on his line, behind or beside him, he must pick it up and chase IT around the circle or even through the circle. IT tries to reach the place in the circle left vacant before its rightful occupant can return to reclaim it. The circle players raise their arms to allow both runners to get in and out of the circle.

Variation

If the game is played in a gymnasium where there is a piano, the piano should have a Staff Chart I behind the keys and IT must get to the piano and play the note that he has laid down before the Note-child gets to the piano to play it first. Then whoever gets to the staff line first is "in" and the one left out is IT.

LEARNING GOAL: Memory training. (Association of keyboard and staff in the variation.)

FARMER IN THE DELL
(A whole note in the measure)

MUSIC: Singing to the tune of "Farmer in the Dell."

EQUIPMENT: Large cutout symbols (four quarter notes, two half notes, large dot, quarter rest, half rest, whole rest, signature of 4/4 time; a piece of rope as long as the height of a staff; colored chalk.)

GAME: Any number of children can play. The group forms a ring on the music-staff playing field. One child represents the Measure in 4/4 time. He places the two cutout fours, one above the other to the right of the treble clef. He then lays the rope at the right end of the staff, forming a vertical edge, a bar-line, at the right side. With the leader's guidance, he makes four vertical strokes at right angles to the lines in the treble staff and also to the left of the rope edge. These marks must be far enough apart to form four sections, each of which will represent one beat; a child with arms and legs spread out should be able to straddle these four sections, or at least feel that he can occupy

FIG. 67. This Measure gets four counts.

120

all of them at once. Measure stands in the center and occupies the four sections. After these preliminaries, everyone sings:

> This Measure gets four counts,
> This Measure gets four counts,
> Heigh-ho the derri-o,
> This Measure gets four counts.

> The Measure takes a Whole Note,
> The Measure takes a Whole Note, etc.

Measure chooses a child wearing a whole-note symbol. Now Measure joins the circle while Whole Note spreads his hands to show that he too owns the whole measure and the four sections. He tries to straddle his legs over them.

Now he will choose two Half Notes who will each occupy two of the blocked-out sections made with the chalk marks. They will stand below the Whole Note who still owns all four sections. Everyone sings:

> The Whole Note takes two Half Notes,
> The Whole Note takes two Half Notes, etc.

Then—

> Each Half Note takes two Quarter Notes,
> Each Half Note takes two Quarter Notes, etc.

If there are many children, proceed after several experiences with the game to:

> Each Quarter takes two Eighth Notes, etc.

If the leader decides not to go as far as Eighth Notes he may continue in this manner, after the Half Notes have chosen their Quarter Notes:

The first Half Note steps out and leads the singing of this verse:

> The Half Note takes a Dot, (repeat) Heigh-ho, etc.

The Half Note, holding hands with his Dot, pushes away three of the Quarter Notes. Half Note and Dot can remove any three of them. Then the Half Note, the Dot, and the remaining Quarter Note arrange themselves in the four sections, the Half Note occupying the first two, the Dot the third section, and the Quater the last. Half Note and Dot hold hands.

The leader can develop this game to include the rests by adding a small new part each week. Each Quarter will then choose a Quarter Rest. Two Quarter Rests will choose a Half Note Rest. Then the two Half Note Rests or the two Quarter Rests and the one Half Note Rest will choose a Whole Note Rest, who replaces all of them. (See p. 186.)

Now everyone circles around him singing:

The Whole Note Rest stands alone (Heigh-ho, etc.)

It is best to clear the staff of the other symbols when introducing the rests, so that the Half Note Rest can stand above the third line and the Whole Note Rest can stand just below the fourth line. Even though this knowledge has formerly seemed beyond the grasp of children, it is so easy to demonstrate in this graphic way that it would be a shame to omit it because of our preconceived notion of its difficulty.

LEARNING GOAL: Time-value concepts.

FEELING THE BEAT

For a quarter note, slap another player lightly on the back or hand, at the same time swinging the upper part of the body to the left.

For a half note, slap lightly on the first swing of the body to the left. Continue to hold the hand down while you swing to the right. Without lifting the hand for the second swing, allow the heel of the hand to slide slightly, i.e. to respond sympathetically, to the swinging of the upper part of the body. When

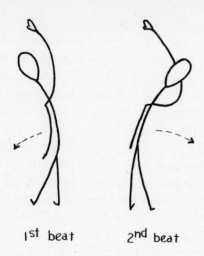

1st beat   2nd beat

Fig. 68.   Feeling the Beat: Half Note.

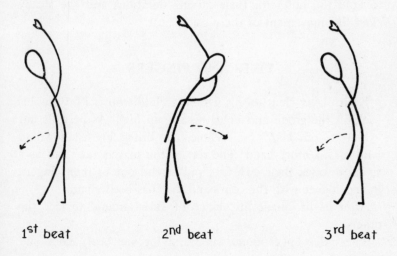

1st beat   2nd beat   3rd beat

Fig. 69.   Feeling the Beat: Dotted Half Note.

interpreting the time-value in this physical fashion, bend from the waist first to the left and then to the right. The hand goes down on the first swing to the left and remains in place during the second swing which is to the right. Avoid any tightness— every movement must have a loose, free swinging quality. The hand does not press, but loosely and gently responds to the swinging. (Fig. 68.)

For the dotted half, slap slightly on the first swing and continue to hold the hand down in contact with the other player— "he who gets slapped." As before, the hand may slide almost imperceptibly along with the remaining two swings. (Fig. 69.)

For the whole note, follow the same directions, except that after the first light slap, the hand is held down lightly for the remaining three swings. (Fig. 70.) An eighth is a light pat with two adjacent fingers held closely together—index and middle fingers. (Fig. 95B, p. 198.)

LEARNING GOAL: The coordination between the poise needed to hold the notes for their varying durations and the steady clock-like movement of the musical beat.

FISTS AND FINGERS

Each player clenches his fist. One child who is IT turns his back on the group and holds his fist up high. As he calls out "Quarter" or "Half" or "Whole," he brings his fist down to land on his other hand. The rest of the players take this as a signal to open their own fists and extend one or more fingers, in accordance with the command that has been given.

After he has made his choice IT turns around to face the others.

The index finger alone will stand for one beat; index and middle finger will represent two beats. All four fingers without the thumb stand for four beats. If IT has called "Quarter," a

1st beat 2nd beat   3rd beat 4th beat

FIG. 70.   Feeling the Beat: Whole Note.

The hand remains in place for the duration of each note; the body bends at the waist from side to side to indicate the musical beat. The objective is the coordination between the poise of one and the movement of the other.

player with only one finger extended wins and becomes IT. If "Half" was called, a player with two fingers wins and trades places with IT; if a whole note has been called for, the player with four fingers extended becomes IT.

LEARNING GOAL: Time-value concepts and instantaneous response.

FOLLOW THE LEADER I

FORMATION: The players form a line at the right of the Leader rather than a single file behind him.

GAME: The Leader steps on each line and space and stamps a certain rhythm on each as the others try to imitate his movements. He may go back to a space or line below if he wishes, but

125

in general he must proceed up the staff. Try to sound the pitch on an instrument and encourage the children to sing along. Anyone who fails to imitate the Leader's rhythm or number of hops, steps, or jumps on each line or space must go to the extreme right of the line.

The player next to the Leader may then challenge the Leader to imitate a rhythm and if he fails, the Leader goes to the right end of the line and the challenger becomes the new Leader.

FOLLOW THE LEADER II

FORMATION: The players stand in single file below the staff.
GAME: The Leader is allowed to jump to three different lines (or spaces) in any order. Each player in the line *behind him* tries to repeat his jumps correctly. Anyone failing goes to the end of the line.
LEARNING GOAL: Training the musical memory.

FORFEITS

EQUIPMENT: Small cutout notes or, as second choice, squares of music paper marked with a note (whole, half, dotted half, quarter, or two joined eighths.)

PROCEDURE: Pay a forfeit of four points with a whole note, a forfeit of three points with a dotted half, two points with a half, one point with a quarter or two eighths.

At the beginning of a game that calls for forfeits, give each player two each of the above symbols. When the scores are settled, the winner can ask the losers to pay these additional forfeits.

1. Crawl along the F, G, or Middle C line on all fours.
2. Hop on one foot on every line, up and down the staff.
3. Hop, squatting like a frog, on every line, up and down the staff.

4. Hop up the lines, holding the other foot with your hand.
5. Indoors, wriggle on your stomach along the F, G, or C line.
6. Pretend to ice skate on the lines.
7. Do a dance along a line or space.

Besides being used as a part of many games, "Forfeits" may be played as a special little game in itself.

Write each of the suggested penalties and others you may devise on separate slips. Put them into a bag and let everybody draw for one. The most humorous performance wins.

LEARNING GOAL: Ingraining the mental staff picture, with emphasis on the landmarks, F, C, and G.

G-G-G, COME GET ME!

FORMATION: A Note-child stands on a line in the treble clef, while the others stand below and at the side of the bass staff.

GAME: Lineman must know the names of the lines with which he will deal. The game demands that he stand on a line and call the name of a line three times, for example: "E, E, E! Come get me!"

If he really is standing on E, the others may come and try to tag him, but if he can get to a safety line such as the F-line in the bass they may not tag him. These lines may be changed by common consent.

However, if he is calling "E, E, E!" and is not standing on E, the others must not be fooled; they must not make a move toward him. As the pursuers make a start toward him when they should have known better, they become Linemen with the original Lineman. Together they cry the name of a line three times and if they are really standing on that line, the others may try to catch them. If they get to a safety line before anyone tags them, they continue calling out the name of a line.

LEARNING GOAL: Preparation for staff reading.

G-MAN (for very young children)

For those who know only the G line and the F line—and the very youngest learn that right away because they are marked by their clefs—the Lineman calls "G, G, G! Come get me!" He can fool the others by standing on the space above or below the line G. If the others below the staff, standing at the sides, make a move toward him when he is standing on a space instead of line G, they become G-men too, and try to catch others.

G-G, PULL AWAY!

FORMATION: One player stands on Middle C; he is IT. All the others stand on bottom line G.

GAME: IT chants on the pitch of a G, "G-G, pull away! If you don't come, I'll pull you away!"

After he says this, all run to get to treble line G. Anyone caught by IT helps to catch the remaining ones. G is the only safe line in this game. (If the group is older—seven or eight—any G could be safe, such as the fourth space in the bass.) First one caught becomes IT. Other safe lines and spaces of the same name may be chosen, all B's, or D's, etc.

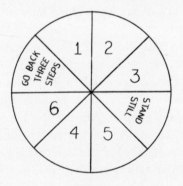

FIG. 71.

Listening to the octave relationship, associating several places on the staff with the same name.

FIG. 72.

GAMEBOARD

EQUIPMENT: A spinner made by pinning a cardboard arrow in the center of a piece of cardboard on which a wheel with eight segments has been drawn. The segments are numbered up to six; and the remaining segments marked, "Stand still" and "Go back three steps."

GAME: Each player is a "man" on the gameboard which is the playing field. Before taking his turn, each player spins the arrow and makes the indicated number of moves, always counting his starting place as Number One. All players begin at bottom line G.

If a player lands on the same line or space as another player, he goes back to the starting place unless he lands on F, Middle C, or G.

Variation

A human spinner may be improvised. One child acts as the Spinner and moves his finger around in a circle as he closes his eyes and finally points at a wheel drawn as described above. He also counts everyone's moves and sees that these are made correctly.

This game may also be played on a cardboard staff with small movable notes instead of with children on the playing field.

LEARNING GOAL: Preparation for interval relationships and general familiarity with the staff.

GAME OF SILENCE (Inspired by a game developed by Montessori)

Each child is given a musical alphabet name and told which line or space is his on the playing field. One child is chosen to be Whisper.

Players stand below the staff, eyes shut tightly, and absolutely quiet. There must be perfect silence, otherwise no one will be able to hear Whisper when he names the line or space to be occupied. Ears must be sharp to pick up the soft sound of each name whispered, and as one child recognizes his, he opens his eyes and tiptoes to his station, but so noiselessly that the others do not hear him. Cutout notes may be given to each to lay down on the staff beside him as he takes his position.

When all have been summoned to the staff, the children close their eyes again. Then Whisper gives the cue for their return by again naming their lines and spaces, and one by one, like the Arabs, "they silently steal away" back to their seats or starting point.

Variation

If this game is played indoors where there is a piano, the players are to go to the piano on their way "home" (back to the starting place) and play their note, but the piano key is to be depressed without making a sound. This gives a sensation of control that is valuable for a future pianist to experience.

LEARNING GOAL: Cultivation of keenness in picking up a cue; preparation for the discipline and control necessary for playing or singing very softly (pianissimo); staff reading.

GRAB BAG

EQUIPMENT: A large bag to serve as a grab bag, twenty-one small squares of paper cut out of a music tablet, Grand Staff of ten lines appearing on each piece of paper.

GAME: There are altogether twenty-one different lines and spaces on the staff, each of which must be marked with a note on a separate slip of music paper. The notes may be quarters, half notes, dotted half notes, or whole notes. When the collection is complete, the pieces of paper are folded up and dropped into the bag. Each player now gets a turn to draw one out of the bag. The longest note on the highest line or space wins. Each child must slap himself the number of times suggested by the number of beats in the note—once for a quarter, twice for a half, etc.

LEARNING GOAL: Staff reading and time-value concepts.

GREAT WALL

The B-C-D territory on the staff is the Great Wall. Middle C is the Guard. Chalk lines may be extended a few feet on each side of the staff to allow greater width for the activity that is to take place in this territory. That means that the first line E in the treble clef is extended beyond the staff in both directions, left and right of the staff. The top line A of the bass clef is also extended to the left and right of the staff.

The goal is the top line F of the treble clef. All the players are at the starting line which is bottom line G in the bass. When Guard calls, "The enemy is coming," the players at starting line G, try to cross the Great Wall without being tagged by Guard. He may not leave the wall, which is the strip between the bass and treble staves, extended by the chalk lines.

Anyone tagged by Guard joins in trying to capture the

players who are trying to get across. The attempts to storm the wall and get to the top line of the treble are always made from the same starting line, G.

The game ends when all the players have been recruited as guards for the Great Wall.

LEARNING GOAL: Preparation for staff reading, with emphasis on the area between the bass and treble staves.

HARMONICA PETE

One day, five-year-old Peter brought a harmonica to music class. Knowing he would be disappointed if he had no chance to use it, I asked him to hold it so that the low notes would be at his left, just as they are on the piano.

He practiced blowing a very low note, a "middle" note, and a very high note. The rest of us stood below the staff, forming a line and holding hands. When he blew a low note, we ran to the bottom of the staff, still holding hands. When he blew a high note we ran to the top of the staff. If he then blew a "middle" note we stepped backwards down to the middle of the staff. Then he played a low note at the end of the keyboard and a high one at the right, as we all ran first to the bottom of the staff and then to the top.

LEARNING GOAL: Association of low tones with lower part of the Grand Staff and the left side of the piano keyboard; association of high tones with the upper part of the staff and the right side of the keyboard. An immediate physical response to pitch in terms of staff and instrument.

HEAVY, HEAVY HANGS OVER

EQUIPMENT: Note cards, each showing one note on the Grand Staff (bass and treble).

GAME: One child is appointed Sheriff, another Judge. All but these two receive note cards. They must not be watched by Sheriff and Judge as they place themselves on the line or space shown on each card. The cards are then collected, shuffled, and handed to the Sheriff. The Judge must sit facing the children on the staff.

The Sheriff now holds one of the note cards over the Judge's head and says, "Heavy, heavy hangs over your head."

FIG. 73.

The Judge says, "High or low?"

If the card shows a note on the bass clef, Sheriff answers, "Low." If the note is on the treble, he answers, "High," adding "What shall we make the owner do?"

The Judge names the punishment, which should be amusing in nature. For example, "Crawl on the G line on all fours!"

"Hop up the staff holding one leg."

"Pretend you're a bullfrog and jump up and down the lines!"

"Take three hops in spaces and then jump as far as you can." Etc.

133

The children know for whom the punishment is intended because they compare their own positions with that of the note on the card.

LEARNING GOAL: Staff reading; comparison of staff locations.

HIDDEN NOTES

EQUIPMENT: One small note cut out of black sponge rubber or a rubber heel, or a small ball (Ping-pong size).
Staff Chart I placed behind the keys on the piano.

FORMATION: All the players except IT take specific places on the staff; IT stands near the piano. He closes his eyes, turns his back to the other children, and throws the ball toward them. The one who gets the ball hides it in his hand, and all stand with hands clenched together.

IT plays the sounds of the places occupied by the children, describing as he does so, the staff location of the tone he is playing.

"Second space, G clef" or "Third line, F clef," for example. He is guided by the Staff Chart I.

If IT can guess the child holding the "note" before his third or fourth try, the holder of the note becomes IT.

Variation

With a five-year-old group, the leader can be IT.

LEARNING GOAL: Association of staff location with sound and keyboard. Familiarity with staff and keyboard.

HIDE AND SEEK

EQUIPMENT: Small note cards (each bearing a note of a different time-value on a specific line or space of the Grand Staff.

GAME: Only a small percentage of the group is given a small note card to hide. One player is chosen to be IT. He leaves the group, leans against a wall, closes his eyes, and while the others are deciding which of them are to hide the notes, IT starts to count in letter names—ABCDEFGABCDEFGA, etc. until he hears that everyone has settled down. Meanwhile the others have hidden the notes under themselves as they sit on the various lines and spaces of the staff indicated to them by the cards.

Leader's Opportunity

The counting time is a fine opportunity for the leader to introduce the singing of an ascending scale in letter names— CDEFGABC, for instance. She can start IT singing this on the right pitch, or she can ask him to sing it up and down, according to his stage of development. Carried away by the impetus of the game, he will have no consciousness that he is performing a difficult feat.

When IT thinks the group is or should be ready, he calls, "Ready or not, here I come!" If the players are not ready, they answer, "Not ready!" IT then resumes singing the scale in letter names and then flatly announces, "Ready or not, here I come!"

This time he goes to each child and asks, "Is there a note hiding on the first line in the bass clef?" If the answer is a nod "yes," he asks, "Is it a half note?" Players who are hiding notes are not allowed to speak. They nod their heads and swing both arms for the required number of swings if the seeker guesses correctly. They may hum the pitch if they wish.

As soon as IT guesses the identity and whereabouts of the note, he gets the card or symbol. He asks the same questions of each of the children until he gathers in all the notes. The first one discovered becomes IT.

The child who has a card showing a note on the third line in the bass sits on that line on the staff. The leader at the piano plays the sounds of each of the staff locations occupied by the children as they are approached by IT.

LEARNING GOAL: The hiders are forced to remember their note, its time-value, and location. The seeker must identify each line and space. During the counting, the musical alphabet is sung both up and down.

HOPOVERS

Kick-off or Accent

EQUIPMENT: Small beanbags, round pieces of black sponge rubber, a rubber heel, or any round object that can be kicked easily from line to space to line, etc. up the staff. If only one is available, all players will use it and must remember its location at the end of each turn. Giant-sized music paper to mark position of note at end of each turn.

GAME: The first player tosses his "note" (the object to be kicked) onto the first bottom line, then, hopping on one foot to the first line, he kicks it into the first space. Still on the same foot, he hops into the first space and kicks the "note" to the second line, and so on as far as he can go up the staff. If he forgets about the space on each side of the imaginary line (Middle C), if his kicking foot touches the ground, if his hopping foot touches the wrong line, or if he kicks the note to the wrong place, he must leave the staff. Gradually change from the word "kick" to "accent." An accented note in music gets a strong "kick-off."

While the next players have their turn, the one who has just finished must remember where he left off. A music tablet may be kept handy so that each player may have his name or initials written on the line or space where he can begin on his next turn. When his turn comes again, he may be shown this and he must toss the bag or note to the line or space marked with his name.

If the toss is successful, he continues from there. First to reach the top line of the treble wins.

LEARNING GOAL: Dramatizing an accented note, ingraining the mental picture of the staff. Comparison of staff on music tablet with playing field.

Both Feet on F–C–G

Draw two notes on fourth bass line F, Middle C, and second treble line G. On these lines (Middle C is always thought of as an imagined line), it is correct to place *both feet*. All other lines and spaces must be hopped on with one foot. At each turn the note is thrown on suceedingly higher lines and spaces. If the note accidentally lands on any of the above special lines, an extra turn is allowed. One does not hop on the line or space that contains the note, but must pick it up from the line or space below when going up; on the way down, one picks it up from the space or line above.

Observe a space on either side of the magic Middle C line. Jumping back down, remain facing the same way that you started when going up. This is important as it dramatizes the backward descent of the musical alphabet, G-F-E-D-C-B-A-G, etc.

Note Pickup

EQUIPMENT: Eleven small cutout or pipe-cleaner notes; one small black line for Middle C note.

PREPARATION: A note is placed on each line and the black line is put through the note on Middle C.

GAME: First player hops in the spaces only, hopping on one foot and avoiding the small notes placed on the lines. On reaching the top space, he removes the note on the top line, always maintaining his balance on the one foot.

Once he has picked up the note, the player may shift to the

other foot and hop down through the spaces on the one foot, never touching a line or any note on a line.

As he hops he must call out the number of each space—first, second, etc. In the B-C-D section he says, "Below Middle C" or "Above Middle C," then continues, "First treble space, second, third, and fourth." He counts as he comes back down, "Fourth space, third, second, first, above C, below C, bass fourth, third, etc." For younger children who would find it too difficult to hop and count simultaneously, omit counting.

Next player hops through all the same spaces. On reaching the top space, he picks up the note on the fourth line and hops down on the other foot. Each player continues up the entire staff in the same manner, picking up the highest note still on the staff. Anyone bending down to pick up a note that is no longer on the staff is out. The leader plays sounds of spaces as the player hops into them, also the sound of the note he picks up.

LEARNING GOAL: Memorizing the notes that have been picked up.

Stick Pick

EQUIPMENT: Ten black cardboard sticks or strips. One white strip or stick with a note that has a line through it.

GAME: A black stick or strip is laid on each line of the playing field and a white strip with a Middle C note is laid on Middle C.

Each player is required to jump on one foot from space to space, never touching any of these sticks. When he reaches the top stick, he must bend down and pick it up. The next player hops through the spaces and after reaching the top space, picks up the stick on the fourth line of the treble, then returns down the staff, still hopping through the spaces. Each succeeding player must hop through all the spaces, but must remember

138

where the highest remaining stick is. If he bends down to pick up a stick where there is none, he loses his turn to someone else.

On Middle C both the strip and the note must be picked up.

Landing with Both Feet

Using a little note cut out of black sponge rubber, jump through the staff, landing on spaces only and holding the note between the feet. Only one jump is allowed for each space. Dropping the note ends the player's turn.

Carrying on One Foot

The note must rest on top of the foot or shoe and be carried throughout the staff in this position.

Initials

Each child is given a cutout note on which he writes his initials. He may cut out his own note using colored construction paper.

Each player hops through the staff on one foot, landing on each line and space. He may stand as long as he likes on any line to regain balance, but he must stand on one foot as he hops to the top. He places his initialed note on any line or space he chooses. The others must hop over the line or space on which a note is parked.

The F, Middle C, and G lines must remain havens for both feet, so no one may place his notes on these lines. Anyone failing to hop properly does not put his note down.

Variation

There may be an alteration if there is an odd number of children playing. One player hops up the staff and the next player, starting at the top, hops down but remains facing the top line of the staff. Wherever possible the players must try to name every line they hop on. If this is done where a piano is available, the naming takes place to the correct pitch which the leader plays for each hop.

At the Seashore

At low tide the beach becomes as smooth as a floor. Children enjoy digging their fingers into the sand and drawing the lines and clefs of the staff. When they have made a musical playing field in the hard-packed, damp sand, they can play any of the

FIG. 74.

Hopover games in this section. Shells can be used for the "puck" or object to be thrown. The clef can also be outlined with shells, and shells can be used as notes.

LEARNING GOAL: Discrimination between lines and spaces through physical movement and intersensory impressions of the staff.

HOT OR COLD

One child is blindfolded. A note is placed on a line or space. The blindfolded one is led to the bottom line of the staff.

If the staff chart is in place behind the keys of the piano, another child can play the loud or soft tones necessary to guide the blindfolded player. At first the leader should officiate at the piano with some helpers, who will soon learn how to take over this part of the game.

If the child who is blindfolded steps up to the third line in the bass and the note for which he is searching has been placed on the first line in the treble, the corresponding tones are played for all the lines and spaces he steps in, but since he is not near the goal, the notes must be played very softly (pianissimo). As he gets closer to the goal the tones get louder. Mezzo piano (pronounced *metso piano*) means a little louder than soft, mezzo forte (pronounced *metso fortay*) medium loud. "Close to the goal" is forte—loud and "On the spot" is fortissimo (extremely loud.)

The English words for these directions may be used if desired, but children enjoy learning words in foreign languages.

LEARNING GOAL: Control of dynamics and tone consciousness; musical terminology.

HUNTING HE WILL GO

CHARACTERS: Mr. G Clef, Mr. F Clef, and Notes.

FORMATION: Mr. F Clef stands on his own symbol in the playing field. The Notes are with him on different lines and spaces of the bass staff. Mr. G Clef, standing on his clef in the treble staff at the beginning of the game, leaves his station and comes down to the bass staff, hunting for "nice, juicy Notes."

GAME: (MR. G CLEF calls down to Mr. F Clef) Will you give me some of your nice, juicy Notes?

MR. F CLEF: No, I will not! (He proceeds to take a nap.)

MR. G CLEF: Then I'll come down and get me some!

F Clef comes down and passes out little slips of paper on which is drawn either a quarter note, a half note, a dotted half, or a whole note. He slaps each Note that he chooses lightly on the back, once for a quarter, twice for a half, three times for a dotted half, and four for a whole note. Depending on the number of players, he may choose either two of each kind of note or if there are not many players, only one of each. Another pos-

141

sibility would be to allow him to take one quarter, two half notes, three dotted half notes, and four whole notes.

If no paper slips are to be passed out with the written symbol, he may simply give them the right number of light slaps and whisper the name to each Note. He takes them up to his own staff, and they form a line along the G line, hands on the shoulders of the player in front, all facing toward the G clef.

Mr. F Clef wakes up from his nap and seeing his ranks depleted, calls on Mr. G Clef.

Mr. F Clef: Have you seen my nice, juicy Notes?

Mr. G Clef: No, I haven't.

Mr. F Clef: What have you got behind you?

Mr. G Clef (shrugging his shoulders): Just some old skinny Notes.

F Clef (not convinced): "Let me see. They look like my Notes." F tries to guess the time-value of each note. If the Note says his guess is right, F must give him the right number of taps on the shoulder. G Clef tries to prevent this. F Clef may take back to his own staff any Note he can tap. The released Note goes to the F line in the bass.

Variation for More Advanced Group

The game is essentially the same except that in the beginning, the Notes are placed on *specific* lines and spaces of the bass clef. When G Clef takes the Notes to his treble staff, besides making them into various time-values (quarters, halves, etc.) he must also place them on a line or space of the same name in his own staff. This is best done by escorting only one Note at a time so that he can remember the name of each.

When F comes to claim his lost Notes, besides guessing their time-values with the shoulder tapping, he must lead each one to his original place on the staff. This is done by placing each Note on a place of the same name as that occupied in the treble, assuming that the G Clef placed them correctly. If he makes a mistake, the Notes are awarded to G Clef. If G Clef puts any of the Notes in the wrong place in the treble, they return to the bass and belong to F Clef.

LEARNING GOAL: Reading, octave relationships, and time-value concepts.

KEEPING SCORE

Scoring System I

Each child has a sheet of paper on which the following numbers are written in a vertical row at the side of the sheet. (Ample room should be left above and below each number.)

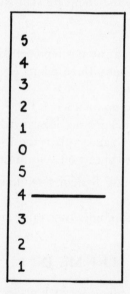

FIG. 75.   Score card.

These numbers represent the five lines of each staff. The zero stands for Middle C. In any game that involves the landing of an object on a staff-line of the playing field, these numbers provide a scoring system which may also be used as a game by itself.

If a player lands his beanbag (or other object representing a note) on the fourth line of the bass on the musical playing field, for example, he would be allowed to draw a staff-line on his paper, beginning at the fourth number from the bottom and continuing horizontally to the right. (See Fig. 75.)

If he lands on Middle C, instead of drawing a line, he creases his paper along the imaginary line indicated by the zero. The game continues until someone has drawn in all the lines for a complete staff. The others add up their scores by counting up the numbers beside which they drew the corresponding staff-lines. The player with the complete staff wins.

Scoring System II

One point scored in a game is represented by a quarter note; two points by a half note; three points by a dotted half; four points by a whole note.

These may be added up for a score. Keep score on large music paper. If a particular line or space is involved, as in Note Hockey or any of the beanbag games, place the time-value symbol on that line or space as it appears on your music-staff scoreboard.

LEARNING GOAL: Scoring System I reinforces the mental staff picture.

Scoring System II combines time-value and reading concepts.

LET ME IN! I

EQUIPMENT: Note symbols for each player. Extra note symbols in a pile for IT to choose from. Cutout numbers for signature (3/4 or 4/4).

FORMATION: A certain number of children stand on each line or on specially appointed lines. This will depend on the number of children playing and on the time signature. If there are only twelve children playing, only a few lines will be used. The players wear their costumes and stand facing away from the clefs.

GAME: The players choose their note costumes. Two children wearing half-note symbols may stand on one line in 4/4 time. If there is a small group playing, all the children may be half notes and only two will stand on each line used. If there is a large group playing, four children wearing quarter notes occupy each line. Any combination that adds up to four counts to a measure is acceptable. For ease in remembering the groupings on each line, it is suggested that the variety be limited at first.

IT chooses a note symbol and runs up and down along the clef edge of the staff, behind the backs of the players standing on the lines. They do not know on which line he will decide to place his note. As soon as one line becomes aware of the fact that IT has placed his note on their line, they must leave their places, run around the staff, and try to get back "home."

Since IT has taken his stand on the line, not all of the players can return. The first ones to return get back on their line, but only those who can still be accommodated without making too many beats may come in.

If IT chooses to place his quarter note on a line which originally contained a Half Note and two Quarters, one of the original Quarters will be left out, since only a Half Note and a Quarter can return. The outcast becomes IT for the next game.

If the note belonging to IT is a half note or a dotted half note, more than one player will be left out. In that case, the old IT chooses his successor. IT may not choose a whole note as no one else can get back to his line.

LEARNING GOAL: Measure concept.

145

LET ME IN! II (for younger children)

Children are divided so the same number may stand on each line, facing away from the clefs. IT runs up and down behind them at the edge of the staff near the clefs and tries to make up his mind where to place the note he carries in his hand. The others all wonder which line he will choose. They are not supposed to look back, but often children in the other lines will wink or point back if they can see out of the corner of their eyes that IT has deposited his note.

As soon as the Notes on a line become aware that IT has chosen their line, they run around the staff and try to get back "home."

Since IT will have taken his place on the line he selected, and there can be no more occupants than there were before, someone will be left out. He becomes IT and the game starts over.

Four children, each carrying a quarter note, can be stationed on each line or on each of the lines the leader wishes to use. F, C, G are always to be included; bottom line G which is easily remembered and top bass line A are good first choices if only certain lines are to be occupied. Each child can think of himself as a quarter note and gradually the more advanced version of the game can be worked in.

LEARNING GOAL: Reading and time-value concepts.

LINE AND SPACE TAG

One player is IT and he can tag anyone who is not on a line. No one may stand still. OR—only F, Middle C, and G can be considered "safe" lines.

LEARNING GOAL: Reinforcing the visual discrimination between the lines and spaces with physical movement, developing co-ordination between fine eye muscles and the large leg muscles, which results in a deeper involvement.

146

MAGIC CARPETS

FORMATION: Children march in single line in a circle on the staff.

GAME: Certain spaces or lines of the staff are designated "magic carpets." These are not to be stepped on. Music is played (or sung), and whenever it stops abruptly, the children who happen to have stepped on the "magic carpet" lines or spaces are eliminated from the larger circle.

If the playing field staff is large enough, they continue to march around in a smaller circle in the center of the staff. Otherwise they would be eliminated entirely or they would merely be required to pay a forfeit.

The trick is to step *across* the "magic carpets." To begin with, use the F, G, and Middle C lines as "magic carpets"; later use other lines and spaces as the forbidden territory.

LEARNING GOAL: Ingraining the staff image. Anything that is forbidden makes a stronger impression than that which is permitted.

MEASURE RULERS (3/4 time)

Cut pieces of construction paper in half the long way. Each strip is now twelve inches long. Make two creases, one four inches from the left edge and the other eight inches from the left edge. In other words, fold into sections of even thirds.

Each section represents one beat in a 3/4 measure. Cut out notes in contrasting colored construction paper and paste or Scotch tape them on according to time-value. A quarter note in the first section may be followed by a half note, but since the half note gets two beats it requires two sections. Therefore the third section of the measure ruler will be left blank. A dotted half note placed in the first left section owns all three sections so nothing more can go in that measure ruler.

147

Children understand property ownership. One can say, "This Note owns three properties," pointing to each section. "Even though his house covers only one property, no one may build on the others because they belong to him." (See Figs. 67, 77, 78, 79.)

Similar measure rulers may be made for other time signatures; for instance, 4/4 would be folded into four sections. Older children, who have already started to study an instrument, can

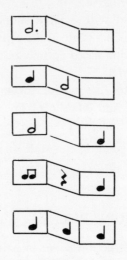

FIG. 76. Measure rulers.

make these rulers for 6/8 or any other time desired. Four measure rulers can be taped together to make a four-measure phrase, if this is desired. These rhythms should be played on a drum and other instruments, the children swinging the upper parts of their bodies for each beat as they sing and play.

LEARNING GOAL: Understanding the structure of a measure unit in preparation for understanding of the phrase unit; sensing the duration of a measure through a tactile and spatial experience.

148

MIDDLE C, CAN'T CATCH ME!

Several children sit on black strips of paper on the magic Middle C line. (There is an extra supply of these black strips for those who will be tagged during the game.)

The other players stand on the F line in the bass clef (F clef) and the G line in the treble or G clef.

GAME: Players on each clef tease the C's by coming as close to them as they can, taunting them, "Middle C, Middle C, can't catch me!"

The Middle C's may not stir from their places, but they try to reach out and touch the other Notes. Any player touched becomes a Middle C and gets a black strip to sit on. As soon as there is no room to sit on Middle C, use an imagined extension of the magic Middle C line. (A double stretch of the imagination!)

The players cannot retreat beyond their original stations. If these lines are too close to Middle C, choose the line below the F line and above the G line, just far enough away to be a little out of reach but not too far.

New Middle C's try to tag the teasing faction. Game ends when everyone is a Middle C.

LEARNING GOAL: Review of the staff landmarks, F line, Middle C, and G line. Dramatization of Middle C's special placement.

MOVING NOTES

EQUIPMENT: Specially tuned Autoharp or a piano; bell to sound as a signal. Large size music paper; Staff Chart I behind piano keys; Staff Chart II drawn on large wrapping paper or wide shelf-lining paper.

GAME: One child is chosen to be the Orchestra Leader. He assigns each player to a seat on a specific line or space, marking each name and position on the music paper he holds in his hand.

At a signal from the Orchestra Leader—a tone played on the piano or specially tuned Autoharp—the Notes rise and run around the staff two or three times, but each must remember his exact position on line or space. The Leader signals again and each Note must return to his place. The Orchestra Leader checks them off against his official list on the music paper and those who are "lost" have a point against them.

Variations

The leader can give each one a piece of music paper with his note written on the Grand Staff. This accustoms the child to form a vivid image and also to focus on the staff whether it be large or small. Encourage children to come to the instrument and play their notes at some point in the game.

LEARNING GOAL: Instrumental application of staff reading. Memory training; transference from the large playing field staff to the music pad.

MUSICAL CHAIRS

EQUIPMENT: Quarter notes cut out of black construction paper, cardboard painted black, or best of all, cut out of plywood with a jigsaw. Phonograph if available. Optional: Staff Charts I and II, also Strip Staff inserted in the piano keyboard. (See pp. 20–29.)

GAME: The children note the resemblance of the quarter notes to chairs—the round seat, the straight back. Place the quarter notes on the staff, one for each child except one. Start the music (phonograph, piano, or just someone singing). The players march around the outside of the staff in time with the music. While the music is going on, no one is allowed to step on the staff. When the music stops abruptly, everyone scrambles for a "chair."

Since the paper quarter notes tear easily if several children pounce upon them at once, each child must run first to the line or space on which a note has been placed. As he stands on this line or space he picks up the note and holds it. One person will be left without a "chair."

If the children have had some experience with the staff chart at the piano, they should come to the piano and play "themselves" by following their line or space on the staff chart into the corresponding piano key. Each time the game resumes, one more "chair" is withdrawn. Last player to remain in the game wins.

LEARNING GOAL: Concentration on the lines and spaces and sharpened visual focus on the staff brought about through competition.

NICKNAMES

EQUIPMENT: Colored chalk or five yardsticks to block off four sections representing the four counts or beats in 4/4 or common time. These can be laid out on the playing field music staff or anywhere else.

Make the sections small enough for a child with arms and legs stretched to their fullest extent to feel that he is occupying them, and yet each section must be large enough for two children acting as eighth notes to squeeze into it. Cut out black paper note symbols. Any instruments for rhythm. Pipe cleaners of four different colors taped together as in Conducting Design for 4/4, p. 109.

GAME: Four children, each bearing a quarter note, take their places, one in each section. Others start swinging both arms, like the ropes of a swing. Each swing indicates the pulse or beat. Each child gets a turn to sing a one-syllable nickname of his own and join in. The names must be only one syllable long—Pete, Fred, Kate, Pam, for instance. They sing and swing one name four times for *one* measure, then do it for four complete measures to get the feel and duration of a four-measure phrase, or they may sing and swing a different name for each measure. Someone may conduct as in Cheer Leader 4/4 p. 103 during this swinging and singing.

The four children go to the piano or any other instrument and one child at a time plays the same rhythm on any tone. They should sing the same one-syllable nicknames to each quarter and swing the right hand while playing at the keyboard with the left. Swing back on one, forward on two, back on three, forward on four. "Pete, Fred, Kate, Pam," or "Pete, Pete, Pete, Pete."

Two children leave and the remaining ones change into half-note costumes. They now occupy two sections each by straddling them with their legs, from the beginning of one section to the end of the other. Now they sing their nicknames—still the one syllable, but stretched out to fill the time-value of two swings. Everyone swings and joins in chanting the names to the swings. "Pe-ete, Pa-am"; now they take turns in going to an instrument and playing, swinging, and singing the names on any tone. They sing "Pe-ete, Pa-am." They step as they swing backward and wait while they swing forward.

FIG. 77.

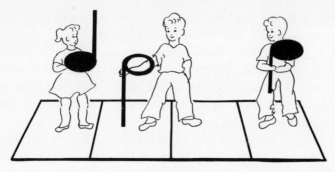

FIG. 78.

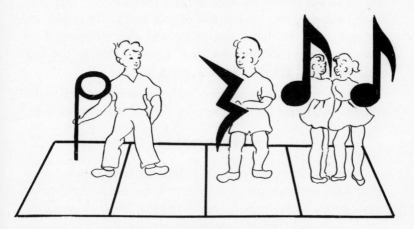

FIG. 79.

One Half Note leaves and in place of him a Dot and a Quarter enter the sections.

At first, the Half Note and the Dot sing a nickname like "Ja-a-ack" for three swings. The Quarter will sing "Jim." All now join in to sing, "Ja-a-ack, Jim." While singing "Ja-a-ack," swing back, forward, back; then sing "Jim" on the last forward swing. This rhythm should be tried on a single tone at the piano.

The dotted half can also be represented by one child holding a half note to which a large dot is attached by means of two

153

pieces of Scotch tape, the two glued sides stuck together so the opposite sides are smooth. (Fig. 77.)

The Quarter Note should exchange places with the Dotted Half Note and stand on the first space, the Dotted Half on the last three. The same routine should be followed. They sing and swing, "Jim! Ja-a-ack," four times, then go to the piano or other instrument to play this rhythm.

Now they leave and one child comes in as a Whole Note. He straddles all four spaces and stretches out his hands to indicate his sole ownership of the property. He makes his one-syllable nickname last for four swings. "Bi-i-i-ill." All "step and swing," stepping only on the first of four swings. They play on any tone with one hand and swing with the other, for four measures. Swing back, forward, back, forward. Play on the first of the backward swings. (See Fig. 67, p. 120.)

LEARNING GOAL: Rhythmic coordination needed for feeling the beat and measuring both the time-values and the measure unit.

NOTE HOCKEY

EQUIPMENT: Paper ovals, each a different color, representing notes; long sticks or plywood quarter notes for hockey sticks; cutout paper Easter eggs, Valentine hearts, Xmas decorations, etc., to suit each holiday season (instead of the oval notes). Large, long music staff to serve as scoreboard.

GAME: One child is Referee, another is Scorer. The others stand below the bottom G line. Referee may cry, "Push to spaces!" whereupon everyone hopes that his oval will land on a space. Referee may cry, "Push to lines!" and the lines become the goals.

Scoring

The scoring is the most important part of the game. The scoreboard music staff is divided into long measures for each player. If a note lands on the bottom (first) line of either bass or treble staff, score a quarter note as one point for that player. Score a half note for a player landing on a second line; a dotted half note is worth three points for anyone landing on a third line and a whole note, four points, for anyone landing on a fourth line. No points for top line or Middle C. (Rest symbols may be given for these.)

If scoring for space landings, allow a quarter note for a first space, a half note for a second space, a dotted half for a third space, and a whole note for a fourth space.

LEARNING GOAL: Concentration on the staff and on time-values.

NOTES AND MUSICIANS

FORMATION: Divide the group into two teams—the Notes and the Musicians. The Notes now take their places on the bottom line in the bass clef. The Musicians face them on the top F line in the treble.

GAME: The Notes secretly choose a single note they will represent. Next, the two sides advance toward the Middle C line. Notes stand on the space below Middle C, Musicians on the space above. The Musicians try to guess what note the opposite team represents.

As soon as they guess correctly, the Notes run back to their starting point as the Musicians chase them. Any Note caught is escorted to the line or space that he represented. (If the playing field staff is small, he will stand on an imaginary extension of his line or space at the side of the staff.) That ends the first "inning."

The two teams re-form as before and a new note is secretly chosen by the Notes.

After a certain number of Notes are caught, the Musicians play an original tune composed of the Notes they have caught.

A staff chart at the piano aids them in locating the notes on the keyboard.

If the game is played out-of-doors, the leader can give the pitch for the notes on a pitch pipe, or re-tuned Autoharp. (See p. 51.) Out-of-doors, more distance between the starting points of the two teams can be obtained by measuring off an equal distance on either side of the staff. Think in terms of additional unseen lines above and below the ordinary staff-lines. Observe the same space between the imaginary lines as exists between the lines of the staff.

LEARNING GOAL: Familiarity with notes on the staff. Opportunity to create tunes with these notes. Introduction to the unseen lines on either side of the staff (leger-lines) below the bass bottom line and above the top treble line. This prepares the way for the concept of leger-lines above and below the staff.

NOTES IN THE MEASURE (3/4 time; based on the folk game, Squirrels in the Trees)

FORMATION: (3/4 time) This measure with its three even beats is represented by the three sides of a triangle. The figure is formed by three children, arms thrust straight out at the sides,

FIG. 80. Notes in the measure—3/4 time.

each just touching his neighbor's fingers; each complete span represents one side of a triangle.

Within each group stands a Note wearing the dotted half note cutout on his head or over his arm. Four other such groups are formed and stand around the staff playing field or in any large room. There should be two odd players without a measure in which to stand. One should wear the symbol of a half note and the other a quarter-note symbol. Each side of a triangle may wear a quarter-note symbol.

GAME: At a clap or other signal from the leader, all Dotted Half Notes run out of their measures and try to get into a different measure. At this time, the Half Note and his partner, the Quarter Note, run together and try to get into a measure that has been vacated.

If they are successful, the winning Half Note becomes a Dotted Half; his partner, the winning Quarter Note, takes his place as one side of the living triangle. The displaced Quarter Note is now out in the cold. The Dotted Half Note left out of his triangle is demoted to the rank of Half Note. He trades costumes with the Dotted Half and joins forces with the homeless Quarter Note.

At the end of the game, the children make up a song in three-four time. The Dotted Half in each measure touches each side of the live triangle for each beat or swing. The homeless Half and his partner the Quarter Note, swing both arms backward and forward to each beat. They also sing (to the nursery tune of—"Pussy cat, pussy cat, where have you been?"):

> Dotted Half, Dotted Half, show us your face,
> Quarter and Half Note have taken your place.

NOTES IN THE MEASURE (4/4 time)

FORMATION: Four children hold their arms out straight and each forms the side of a square. Each wears a quarter note sym-

157

bol. (Use the elastic cord to hold it on.) Other groups of four make similar squares, each of which stands for a measure in four-four or common time. It would be advantageous to have four measures so that at the end of the game the children could sing a simple song, and not only feel each side of the square, that is, the four even beats in a 4/4 measure, but also feel the four-measure phrases ("Yankee Doodle" is made up of such phrases; the first section consists of two four-measure phrases.)

FIG. 81. Notes in the measure—4/4 time.

Within each square will stand a Whole Note wearing his symbol. A Dotted Half Note and a Quarter Note stand outside the squares.

GAME: At a given signal, a clap or whistle-blow from the leader, all the Whole Notes leave their measures and run to get into a new measure. The Dotted Half Note and his partner, the Quarter Note, seize a vacated measure if they can. The winning Dotted Half Note becomes a Whole Note. The displaced Whole Note is demoted from a four-star general to a three-star, four counts to three counts. In other words, our four-beat note becomes a three-beat note.

The winning Quarter Note becomes a side of the square (since each side represents a quarter), as the new Whole Note takes out one of the old sides of the square that he now occupies. This quarter-note beat (a former side of the measure) becomes the Quarter Note partner of the outside note, the new Dotted Half.

At the end of the game, the group sings a simple tune and the Whole Note in each square touches each side of his square on each beat. Sing slowly "Yankee Doodle," for instance.

Touch a different side for each syllable except in the words, "po-ny." Here, each syllable is worth two sides. "O-ni," also gets two sides for each syllable.

LEARNING GOAL: Time-value concepts through kinesthetic experience.

PASS IT TO ME! I (A circle game)

EQUIPMENT: A note cut out of sponge rubber or other material more durable than paper.

GAME: The players form a circle around the staff, taking up positions on lines or spaces. A center player, who must locate the note that will be passed around, stands in the center of the staff on Middle C. The circle players keep their hands behind their backs as they pass the note to each other. The object is to direct the attention of the center player to one part of the circle while the note changes hands in another.

If there are too few children to make a circle effect and still have players in each line, reduce the number of lines used.

When Middle C thinks he has discovered the holder of the note, he calls out the position of the player on the staff (first line treble, for instance) or the alphabet name if he can. If his guess is correct, he changes places with the player caught with the note.

PASS IT TO ME! II (A tag game)

FORMATION: Players are scattered about the staff standing on various lines and spaces. IT is at Middle C near the clefs at the start of the game.

GAME: A small rubber note is passed from one player to another. IT tries to tag the player who has the note. The line or space child who gets tagged while holding the note becomes IT.

The players may pretend to give their notes to a player higher up on the staff and suddenly veer around and throw or pass the note to a player below them on the staff, always trying to confuse IT. Players can run only along their own line or space, but they can pass their note to another player even while being chased by IT along their line or space.

With children old enough to remember their musical names, the catching of the note should be accompanied by a calling out of the name of the line or space child who has received it.

Variation

Indoors, a leader playing the sounds at the piano can add the auditory dimension to the games; outdoors, the converted Autoharp will accomplish the same purpose.

In this case, IT must try to sing on pitch the name of each note-child he tags.

LEARNING GOAL: Personal relationship to the notes and the staff.

PAT ON THE BACK

FORMATION: One of the players is chosen to be IT. He stands in the center of the staff with his eyes closed and his face covered with his hands.

Other members of the group are divided into Half, Dotted Half, and Whole Notes. Each chooses the line or space where he will stand, but IT is not allowed to look. A record of the note chosen by each child can be kept on music paper.

GAME: The players take turns in running up to IT to pat him on the back to indicate their time-value, according to the method of feeling the beat described on pages 122 and 124.

IT tries to guess the identity of each tapper, his time-value and position on the staff. (The leader can limit the guessing to one or two of these.) If IT guesses correctly in three tries, the Note must act out his time-value along his line or space in the step-and-swing manner described on p. 75. If IT fails, he must act out the correct time-value along the line or space of the Note whose identity he failed to guess.

LEARNING GOAL: Time-value concepts and rhythmic coordination; personal association with various staff locations.

PIANO PLAYER AND NOTE

FORMATION: At the beginning of the game, all the children stand below the staff.

GAME: One child is chosen by the alphabet counting-out to be the Piano Player. He is sent off and must not listen while the rest of the group choose someone to be the Note. The whole group gathers in a tight mass about this child whose identity is not yet divulged. (See p. 60.)

After the conference, Piano Player returns and asks, "May I please see Note?"

The group answers, "Not now."

"Where can I find Note?" asks Piano Player. The group answers, "On the fifth line in the treble." (Or whichever line they have chosen for Note to stand on.) The group then moves up the staff all together, counting the lines of the staff. As soon as they reach the specified line, they break away from Note who remains standing on his line while the others form a circle.

Piano Player tries to get at Note but may do so only after the circle is formed. Piano Player tries to chase Note in and out of the circle. The circle children try to help Note by keeping Piano Player out of the circle and by letting Note through whenever he has to get out to escape his pursuer.

Game ends when Piano Player tags Note and plays "him" on whatever instrument is available.

LEARNING GOAL: Staff-line relationships.

POST OFFICE

CHARACTERS: Postmaster, Bass Mailman, Treble Mailman, Tenants.

EQUIPMENT: Re-tuned Autoharp, large Staff Chart II on the wall; one "letter" for each tenant—slips of music paper (including both staves) with one note of a different time-value (quarter, half, dotted half, or whole note), on different staff locations. Optional—a piano with Staff Chart I behind the keys. (See Fig. 21B, p. 24.)

GAME: There must be a tenant for each line and space and each tenant is known as Mrs. G or Mr. A, according to the name of his staff location.

Postmaster looks at each slip. If the note is on the bass staff, he hands it to Bass Mailman, who finds the name on the staff chart, sounds the pitch on the piano or the specially prepared Autoharp, and sings it out, "I have a letter for Mr. D."

All the Mr. D's rush up to claim it, but Treble Mailman gives it to the one who was on the line or space that produced that exact pitch.

"Postage due," says the Mailman.

The one who received the letter goes in to see the Postmaster

162

and shows him the "letter." For instance, it might be a slip bearing a dotted half note on third line D in the bass. Postmaster must recognize its name. If he says, "You're Mr. D." (and this is correct) he may add, "I have something for you," and give the recipient of the letter three light slaps on hand, back, or shoulder. If he cannot name the third bass line as D, the one who received the letter gives the Postmaster the three slaps corresponding to the time-value on the "letter."

The game proceeds in similar vein for each "letter."

LEARNING GOAL: Immediate instrumental application of reading experience; comparison of pitch; recogniton of line and space names and time-values.

PRISONER'S "BASS"

EQUIPMENT: Five sticks or unsharpened pencils of one color for the bass team and five of another color for the treble team. These represent the five lines needed to make up a staff for each team.

GAME: Players are divided into two equal groups and take their places above and below the staff. They determine their positions before the game starts by pacing off an equal number of imaginary staff-lines above and below their particular staff—so many paces above the top line of the treble on which the treble team will stand, and so many paces below the bottom line of the bass on which the bass team will stand, facing the opposite team.

Five pencils or sticks of one color are placed on the top line of the treble staff. The other five of a different color are placed on the bottom line of the bass staff. These represent the two goal lines. The object of the game is for the members of each team to capture the sticks belonging to the other team without being tagged, and to make a staff for themselves.

163

If a player *is* tagged, he is put in the enemy's prison, which is the signature, the area beside the clef. For purposes of leaving more staff room, he may be put on the enemy's clef symbol.

If one of his own men can come up to him and touch him without being tagged himself, the prisoner is freed. No one may tag him as he is returning to his own starting place below his staff. No sticks may be taken by a team while any of its men are in prison. Prisoners must be released before more staff-lines are taken from either goal and brought to the opposite territory. The sticks should be kept in two piles. The first team to get enough staff-lines from the enemy to make a staff, wins.

Variation

If the playing area is limited, play with only one team having five sticks. For instance, the treble might not have any sticks; these would be on the bottom bass line. Treble would have to capture them one by one. Members of the bass team would act as guards for their treasure. Prisoners would still be put on the bass clef or signature until rescued by their teammates. The same rules would prevail.

LEARNING GOAL: Familiarity with leger-line concept, signature, and staff structure.

PUSSY IN THE CORNER

FORMATION: One child stands at the left on second line G in the treble. Diagonally opposite stands another child on G (fourth space) in the bass. Two more children occupy staff positions of the same name; one at the left on fourth line F in the bass, balanced by another at the right on first space F in the treble. Each considers himself to be in a "corner."

GAME: One child is chosen to be the Pussy who must go around to each of the players, saying, "Pussy wants a corner." Each pair of players with the same letter name tries to trade places while

Pussy's back is turned. Only players of the same name may exchange corners. If the Pussy can get into an empty corner the player who is put out becomes the Puss.

FIG. 82.

Other lines and spaces may be used later for older groups.

LEARNING GOAL: Familiarity with octave relationships and the different locations for notes of the same name.

RED LIGHT, GREEN LIGHT

FORMATION: One player, who is chosen to be Traffic Cop, stands two imaginary lines above the top line of the treble staff with his back to the other players who stand two imaginary lines below the bottom line of the bass.

GAME: Traffic Cop closes his eyes and calls, "G-F-E-D-C-B-A, RED LIGHT!"

The other players "in traffic" travel from line to space to line up the staff in the same step-wise progression until they are stopped by the red light. Anyone caught moving after the red light has gone on must go back to the beginning. However, any player is considered safe if he assumes certain positions related to the line of the staff he happens to have reached when the traffic stopped.

Fig. 83.

For instance, he will avoid a ticket if he bends down on the first line of either staff and pretends he is tying his shoelaces, in this way relating the bottom line of the treble or bass staff to the lowest part of himself. On the third or middle line of either staff he should jam his hands in his pockets. Caught on the top line of either staff, the player must hold onto his hat as if a strong wind had come up.

First, third and fifth lines of each staff are the only "safe" lines, provided the player is quick enough to relate these lines to the gesture described. The other lines receive just as much attention from the player because he is constantly relating and comparing them to the first, third, and fifth lines. They are thought of as being "above" or "below" these "safe lines" or "safety zones."

After calling, "G-F-E-D-C-B-A, RED LIGHT!", Traffic Cop veers suddenly around, "arresting" those obviously moving or caught out of a "safety zone." These players must go back to their starting place, two imaginary lines below the staff.

"Were you moving?" he asks each of the other players who fancies himself safe.

Player on a first line answers, "Oh, no, Officer, I was just tying my shoelaces."

Player on a third or middle line says, "Oh, no, Officer, I was standing perfectly still with my hands in my pockets."

Player on the fifth or top line answers, "Oh, no, Officer, I was just holding onto my hat."

Traffic Cop checks their statements and gestures to see if they match their staff locations.

The game continues. First one to reach the top of the treble staff wins.

Outdoor Variation

The game is played exactly as above with one added activity for a larger area. At some point after signaling "G-F-E-D-C-B-A, RED LIGHT," and while questioning and examining those who have assumed positions suggesting their staff locations, Traffic Cop may suddenly cry out, "GREEN LIGHT!" At this surprise signal everybody must run around the staff and return to the exact spot and position he has just left. Anyone caught by Traffic Cop must go back to the starting point as well as anyone who comes back to the wrong line and wrong pose. This calls for added vigilance on the part of the officer.

The game continues in the ordinary routine of "Red Light" signals, arrests, pretending to be in "safety zone" positions, etc. until one player reaches the top treble line, holding onto his hat, of course. He then becomes Traffic Cop for the next round of the game.

LEARNING GOAL: Space relationships on the staff understood in terms of one's own body.

RELAYS

EQUIPMENT: Note symbols, two black strips for Middle C.
FORMATION: Divide the staff into two measures and put the same notes in each. Players line up in two single-file columns as in any simple relay.

The first player in each line stands two, three, or four imaginary lines below the staff. (If the lines of the staff are one foot apart, three imaginary lines below the staff would mean three feet below the staff.) The first player of each team has a black strip in his hand.

GAME: On a given signal the first player of each team runs up into the staff, picks up a note from the G line, quickly places it on the Middle C line with the thin black strip beneath it, then returns it to its original position on G.

As he runs back he hands the black strip to the next player on his team, and the game continues until one team is finished.

Variation I

Another simple relay game requires that all the notes be placed on lines. The first player on each team should move them into spaces; the next player must return them to the lines. The relay consists of the alternate placement on lines and spaces.

Variation II

As the group progresses in knowledge and experience, any number of note placements may be devised by an ingenious leader. For example, three quarter notes may be placed on the G line. The object of the game may be to arrange these into the chord C, E, G, each note above the other: one on the Middle C line with its black strip showing, one on the first line of the treble staff, and one on the same G line. The possibilities are limitless.

Variation III

A more advanced task would be to take three notes placed on C, D, E, in the treble for example and place them on C, D, E, in the bass, then return them to their original places. Or one player can put them in the bass and the next return them to the treble.

The leader should play the corresponding sounds whenever possible and the players should sing and name the notes. For best results in this respect, it is wise to have both teams doing the same thing.

LEARNING GOAL: First hand experience with note placements. Association of pitch with staff location.

RUN AROUND I

GAME: Players sit in a circle on lines and spaces around the staff. Odd player is IT and runs around the others. When he touches one of the players, the chosen one must run toward the bottom of the staff, IT is in the opposite direction. First one to get back to the vacant seat wins. Loser is IT as the game continues.

RUN AROUND II

NUMBER OF PLAYERS: Enough to fill each line and space in a vertical or diagonal line up the staff.

FORMATION: Children stand, holding hands, on the lines and spaces in a vertical or diagonal line up the staff, facing away from the clefs.

GAME: One child becomes the Starter. He runs up and down the staff behind the others. Finally he touches two Notes who are standing next to each other. The lower one must run around the bottom of the staff and the higher one around the top, in opposite directions. The one who gets home first is safe; the

FIG. 84.

Starter takes the place of the loser and the loser becomes the Starter. Play two tones that identify the players chosen to run around the staff.

LEARNING GOAL: Recognition of higher and lower tones. Memory training in locating positions on staff.

SPACE CHASE I

FORMATION: Players form a circle on the staff with their arms stretched straight out at the sides, hands touching. These players may stand only on lines of the staff. Two players are chosen for Runner and Chaser.

GAME: The game begins with Runner stooped under the outstretched arms of two circle players on one side of the circle nearest the clefs. Runner must have his feet on a space. Chaser

FIG. 85.

should be in the same position on the opposite side of the staff. Leader signals the start of the chase. Runner must weave in and out but may step only on spaces. Chaser also may step only on spaces.

Runner may also dash across the circle as long as he runs along a space. Chaser must go across by way of the same space. If Chaser catches Runner, Runner joins the circle people standing on the lines. Chaser becomes Runner and chooses a new Chaser.

If the chase gets too long, player standing on the bottom G line may call "Time!" and a new Runner and Chaser can be chosen.

If the group is not large enough for each line to be occupied in circle formation, make the circle smaller by omitting the top treble lines.

SPACE CHASE II

NUMBER OF PLAYERS: Fourteen.

FORMATION: Twelve players stand in two rows on the staff, about five feet apart and facing each other. In each row the players stand on bottom line G, third bass line D, top bass line A, first treble line E, third treble line B, and top line F, in other words on every other line of the staff.

GAME: The two remaining players are the Hunter and the Extra Note. They start the game at a signal from the leader. Extra Note starts to wind in and out between the children, stepping only on spaces. Hunter must follow in his tracks.

Extra Note does not have to run between each two players consecutively. He may make his way between any two in one row. The only requirement is that he step only in spaces and that Hunter follow his exact trail.

If they can, Line Notes should call out the number of the space the Extra Note stepped on (first bass, second, or first treble, etc.) in order to help the Hunter. When Extra Note finishes weaving in and out of the row on one side, he runs between the children in the other row.

FIG. 86.

If he gets through both rows without being caught, he is safe and takes his place in a row of Notes on the bottom line, while the others move up to higher positions in the same formation as before. All except the two who have been pushed off the top line now have a new location and a new name. The Notes pushed off the staff now become the new Hunter and the Extra Note as the old Hunter and Extra Note take over the positions on the bottom bass line.

The winner of the game is the Extra Note if he did not allow himself to get caught or the Hunter if he was successful in catching Extra Note.

LEARNING GOAL: Discrimination between lines and spaces.

2. *INTERMEDIATE GAMES*

BLACK KEY SCRAMBLE

EQUIPMENT: Piano key costumes as described below.

DIRECTIONS FOR MAKING PIANO KEY COSTUMES

White-Key Costumes

Either a sheet of white crepe paper with a hole for the head to come through, a long sheet of heavy paper with white elastic cord through two holes in the top corners, or two white poster-boards strung together like a sandwich board can serve as the white-key costumes. A number of intermediate and advanced games, such as Black Key Scramble, C Major White Keys, and Chromatic Cousins, call for these costumes. Only eight are needed for these particular games, but additional ones may be needed for original games the children may wish to make up when they act out little melodies.

A piece of music paper (always for the purposes of the games in this book, containing both treble and bass staves) should be attached to the front of the costume. A single note should ap-pear on each of the costumes. The above-mentioned games call for the eight notes from Middle C to the C above. Additional notes that occur in favorite tunes or piano primer pieces can appear on the extra white-key outfits as they are needed.

Black-Key Costumes

Sandwich-board arrangements of narrower black cardboard or sheets of black crepe paper with a hole for the head may be used for those acting as black keys. A black paper cutout of a sharp should appear on one side of the costume and a black paper cutout of a flat should be attached to the other side. This is to show that the black keys can be either sharps or flats, depending on their relationship to neighboring white keys.

GAME: Seven children receive a white-key costume marked with a single note from Middle C to the B above. The Whites then arrange themselves in proper alphabetical order, spreading out with C at the left and proceeding up to B on the extreme right, paralleling the actual keyboard.

The remaining children don their black-key costumes and stand apart, waiting for a signal from the Whites.

Whites confer and decide on the signal. They choose a leader. B could automatically be the leader since B is called the leading tone in C major. This arrangement of notes is the scale of C major without the repeated C on top.

The Whites sing the C major scale, each key adding his tone after Middle C starts them off. The Leader may finish the scale each time with the high C. They do this several times. As soon as they have sung the scale the agreed number of times, they stop abruptly; the Black Keys scramble to get into their proper position. Leader may stop the scale-singing by calling, "Black Keys, come in!" At this signal the Blacks scramble madly to get into the openings.

To make these openings more apparent, C and D should not stand too close together, nor should D and E, F and G, A and B. Only White Keys E and F squeeze tightly together to show that

176

they are only a half step apart and therefore have no opening for a Black Key.

After the players understand the placement of the black keys within the group of seven white keys, one more White Key player should be added, the C an octave (eight notes) above middle C. There is no black key between B and C, so B and C stand close together.

The final step is to arrange the players (White Keys) on the staff, each one standing on his corresponding line or space on the musical playing field. Facing the bottom of the staff and spreading out diagonally with the same spacing as before, Black Keys will stand between, and slightly behind, the same White Keys.

Simple songs like "Au Clair De La Lune" and "Frère Jacques" (changing the last Ding-Dang-Dong to be all on middle C) can be sung by the White Keys, each contributing only his own sound to the melody as he bows. He stays bowed down as long as his note lasts. Many original tunes can be composed on the basis of the C major scale represented by the White Key children.

LEARNING GOAL: Dramatizing the keyboard relationships.

C MAJOR WHITE KEYS

FORMATION: Use "Black Key Scramble" arrangement (p. 176) but in addition place each Key on its corresponding staff location in a diagonal line on the musical playing field. (See Fig. 87 *) Notes a whole step apart stand farther away from each other than those that are only a half step apart, such as the pair

---

* Here the figures are arranged on the treble clef, although they can appear, one octave lower, on the F clef. The bass clef is omitted in the illustration only due to space limitations. The constant presence of the entire Grand Staff, bass and treble, is a factor of prime importance in all the activities described in this book; indeed, it is the *Gestalt* of the entire approach.

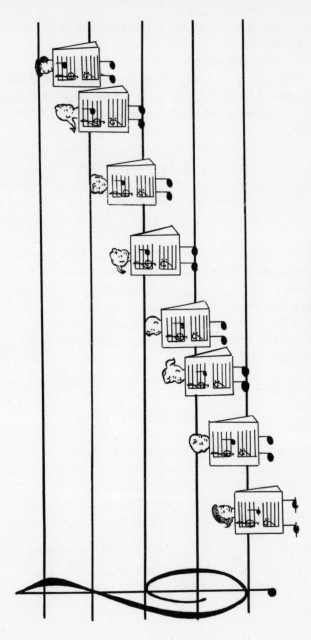

FIG. 87. C major white keys.

E and F and the other pair, B and C. Black Keys are represented only by cards placed on the floor behind every two notes that are a whole step apart.

If the playing field staff is not wide enough to accommodate all the piano keys for this scale in one octave, either chalk in or merely imagine a continuation of each line at both sides of the staff.

GAME: A cutout note is passed from one player to another. In addition to singing and passing the note, each Key who has the note bows as he accepts it.

At the end of the activity, gather around the piano and play the game at the keyboard, each child receiving the note actually playing it.

Variation

Try other patterns such as "Skip one, back up one." Sing and pass the note, following this sequence:

> C to E (who passes it back to D)
> > D to F
> > > E to G etc.

Creative Effort

Children should compose little tunes among themselves.

LEARNING GOAL: A personal experience in C major; introduction to the structure of the major scale.

CALL BALL

EQUIPMENT: Large light ball.

GAME: One player on Middle C with ball; others are assigned to lines and spaces and are instructed to respond to their line or space name—A, B, or C, for instance.

Center player with the ball tosses it into the air calling any alphabet letter from A to G. Note called must catch the ball

179

before it touches the floor. If he succeeds, he becomes the Tosser and goes to Middle C.

LEARNING GOAL: Instantaneous muscular response to the name of a note with which one is identified by location.

CROSS TAG

(Upper Neighbor, Lower Neighbor)

EQUIPMENT: Note cards, each showing a single note on the Grand Staff, should be worn by each player.

FORMATION: Players are assigned to the specific lines and spaces indicated by their cards and they must learn their names thoroughly.

GAME: One player is IT. He calls out a name—A, for example. A runs as IT chases him. If A's upper neighbor B can get in between IT and A, then IT begins to chase B. B's upper neighbor C runs to see if he can get between B and IT. A returns to his place. All the other players may run along their lines or spaces and try to hinder IT from tagging the Note he is chasing.

If IT is successful in tagging a Note, that Note becomes IT and IT takes the name of the Note and returns to his place. Every time there is a new IT, he calls out the name of the Note who must leave his place and be chased.

This game can be played for "lower neighbor" also. In this case, if A's name is called out as the first Note to be chased, his lower neighbor G must try to intercept A and IT. If he does, IT starts chasing G and G's lower neighbor F tries to intercept and becomes the one to be chased. No one else may leave his station, but he may run along his line or space to be of hindrance to IT.

Variation

Runner can call "Help, Upper Neighbor!" and the latter takes a hand in making Runner "safe." Then Upper Neighbor becomes new Runner. Similarly he may call "Help, Lower Neighbor."

LEARNING GOAL: Introduction to the concept of every note having an upper and lower neighbor, a concept of utmost importance in the later study of harmony and counterpoint.

EIGHTHS AND QUARTERS

EQUIPMENT: One pair of eighth notes attached by a bar across the top and four quarter-note cutouts. Four sections as in "Farmer in the Dell."

NUMBER OF CHILDREN: Six.

GAME: Four Quarters stand in their "stalls." Two Eighths, their arms linked together, stand at the side. At a signal from the leader, the Quarters leave their places and march around clapping to each step and to music, all in quarters preferably. (Use Time-Value Parade Marches, pp. 78, 79.)

At a sudden interruption from the leader, who calls "Run home, run!" they run to their sections but the Eighths try to get into one of the sections leaving one of the Quarters out in the cold. Now they act out the rhythm that results. Everyone swings from the waist, from side to side. Each swing represents a beat. To this they slap their thighs for each quarter and gently bring their fingertips together for each eighth. These two contacts of the fingertips take place on one swing. Here are the possible combinations (Fig. 88):

Slap - Slap - Slap - tiptap
Tiptap - Slap - Slap - Slap
Slap - tiptap - Slap - Slap
Slap - Slap - tiptap - Slap

When the coordination for these movements is acquired, increase the number of required coordinations by verbalizing. Use the word Quart' as if it were an abbreviation of "quarter." Example: "Quart' - Quart' - Quart' - eighth - eighth." Try to use all these combinations, through the game; this offers relief from the intense concentration. Follow the same rhythm with "Walk - Walk - Walk - Running," using the word "walk" for the quarter and "running," which requires two running steps, for the two eighths. Aim for a complex of all these suggested responses.

Fig. 88.

After this achievement, use instruments to play these rhythmic combinations on any one tone. Put the symbols down on the playing field and slap each cutout quarter with the hand and pat each eighth note lightly with two adjacent fingers held closely together. (See Time-Value Hand Movements, pp. 196–198.)

LEARNING GOAL: Time-values of eighths and quarters visualized spatially. Developing multiple coordinations.

I SEND

EQUIPMENT: Note cards to be worn by each player.

FORMATION: Put a player on each line and space. Be sure he knows his letter name.

GAME: Player B in the bass clef calls out "B," and B in the treble runs around the staff with bass B running after him. If treble B can get to his own line again, he is safe. Each player in the bass has a turn to call his treble partner out for a run. If the treble partner is caught, he goes to a place of the same name in the bass clef.

LEARNING GOAL: Memory training through physical activity which lengthens the attention span. Octave relationships.

RUNNING FROM THE RESTS

EQUIPMENT: Cutout symbols: quarter, half, dotted half, and whole notes; rest symbols such as small cutout quarter rests, black "sailor hats." Safety pins or masking tape.

FORMATION: Children wearing time-value costumes (quarter, half, dotted half, and whole notes) form a circle around the

FIG. 89. Half note rest.

chaser who wears an assortment of cutout rest symbols. A rest symbol resembling a man's hat, pinned above his waistline, stands for a half note rest (two swings). A rest symbol resembling

FIG. 90. Whole note rest
or whole measure rest.

a man's hat upside down, pinned on the chaser's back below his shoulders, stands for the whole note or whole measure rest. The quarter note rest can be a small cutout carried in his pocket or hand.

The circle is formed a distance away from the staff playing field.

FIG. 91. **Quarter note rest.**

GAME: The chaser, who is called Rest, issues a command to a specific time-value such as: "Half Note, run to the fourth space, G clef!" Half Note tries to get there before Rest catches him.

If Rest catches him, they trade places and the Note becomes Rest. The chaser decorates Note with the correct rest symbol by taping a half note rest above Note's waist or a whole note rest below his shoulders. A quarter note would be handed the quarter note rest symbol.

It may seem wrong to have such a busy Rest, but in playing an instrument the rests are moments of intense preparation for the next entrance of notes which may require a rapid shift of the hand position, silent testing, and elaborate placing of fingers. So a rest in music can indeed be very busy though silent.

A more active-for-all game results if the Notes who are caught help Rest pursue the other Notes when they try to get to the line or space he has chosen for them. The original Rest continues to issue the orders. All chasers must stand away from the Notes in order to give them an even chance to get to their destinations.

LEARNING GOAL: Associating the time-value of notes with their equivalent rest symbols. General staff-reading experience.

SHARP (MUSICAL SPUD)

EQUIPMENT: A soccer ball.

FORMATION: One player called IT stands with the ball at Middle C; the others are appointed to the various lines on the staff.

GAME: Each player must know his name and stand on the corresponding line. IT throws the ball up into the air, calling out an alphabet letter (A to G). The player whose name was called must try to catch the ball. If he succeeds, he tries to hit one of the other players, crying, "Sharp," but he must not move from the place where he caught the ball.

The other players may run along their lines, but not off the lines. Anyone moving away from his line or anyone hit by the ball becomes IT. If no one is hit, the player who last threw the ball remains IT. If the original thrower happens to catch the ball on the fly, he remains IT.

Each time a player becomes IT he has a sharp against him; three sharps and he is out. He stands on the sidelines until someone else gets three sharps; then the first ousted player may come back into the game.

LEARNING GOAL: Reflex-like response that proves identification with an assigned staff location.

SILENT RESTS

EQUIPMENT: Cutout black "sailor hats" to stand for whole rest or half rest; music paper on which the leader is to write each player's name or initials and either a half note or whole note beside the name in order to check on the players later in the game.

Preparation

Only the half rest and the whole rest are used in this game and, as they look alike except for their different placement, it is

185

important to learn to recognize them. Often a whole note rest is used for a whole measure even though the measure does not have four beats. Whether it stands for a whole note (four counts) or a whole measure, it is a small, black, rather thick bar that is placed below and yet attached to, the fourth line in whichever clef it is supposed to represent silence. For children it may be illustrated by a sailor hat turned upside down.

A half note rest is worth just two beats of silence and rests directly on top of the third line (in either clef). It may be represented as a sailor hat in normal wearing position.

The quarter note rest is worth one beat of silence. It is placed rather centrally on either staff, but is not identified by its location on any specific line. Some children say it reminds them of a lightning streak; others of a funny numeral "three" or a letter "W" on its side. (See Figs. 89, 90, 91. Also p. 197.)

GAME: The leader is called Whisper. No one may make a sound as this is another game of Silence.

Each child is given a cutout black "sailor hat" and told whether he is to be a Whole Rest or a Half Rest. He may also be assigned to a special clef. Everyone closes his eyes tightly and after perfect silence is achieved, Whisper touches each child in turn on the shoulder. Each summoned player goes up to the staff and puts his "hat" down, either hanging onto the underside of the fourth line if he is a Whole Rest or sitting on top of the third line if he is a Half. If he has been assigned to a special clef, he makes himself at home in that clef by "hanging his hat" there.

Whisper checks a list he has made. Beside each player's initial or name appears a whole or half note.

If he is a Whole Rest, each player is to stand next to his paper symbol with his feet along the bottom edge of the fourth line (one foot in front of the other); if he is a Half Rest, with his feet along the top edge of the third line. In addition, the Whole-Note Rest "acts out" the placement further by putting elbows

FIG. 92. Boy personifies whole note rest; girl, half note rest.

out, fingertips of both hands together, and holding his arms under his collarbone which will stand for the fourth line; or in imitation of the half-note placement, he holds his arms directly above his "middle" which stands for the third or middle line.

LEARNING GOAL: Discrimination between whole rest and half rest. Imitation of their placement on the staff through gesture, pose, and transference of staff space relationships to one's own body.

SPIN THE WHOLE NOTE

Preliminaries

Children are assigned alphabet names and they are to find their places on the lines and spaces that fit the names. Special care should be taken to learn the assigned names and location. There should be two of each name—one for each clef so there will be more sport in running up to prevent the spinning whole note (a pie plate edged with black to identify it as a whole note) from dropping. In addition, with two sets of Notes, those of the same name can change places at a given signal from the Spinner, who sits on Middle C with the players in a circle around him.

GAME: Spinner on Middle C spins the plate, at the same time calling out, "Whole Note wants to go to _____" (he names one of the musical alphabet letters). The two children sitting on places of that name run to get the plate before it drops. Whoever gets there first, claims it and trades places with the Spinner.

Every now and then, Spinner may call out, "A whole note gets four counts!" At this, all Notes trade places. No one may go to a line or space that has not been occupied before. This automatically develops a musical memory—keeping clearly in mind the Notes that are on the staff at the beginning of the

188

game. The children are also forced to learn a new name for themselves after they have changed places. At other times, Spinner calls, "Whole Note, change clefs!" At these words, Notes sitting in the treble change places with Notes of the same name in the bass and vice versa.

FIG. 93.

(This last element of the game should be omitted unless the group has had experience with interchange between the two staves, treble and bass.)

In each of these exchanges of place, either the one between Notes of different name or between Notes of the same name, the Spinner tries to get into a vacated line or space. The child left out becomes the Spinner.

Anyone who fails to respond correctly or in any way blunders, pays a forfeit by doing something four times: hopping on one foot four times or jumping four times, etc.

LEARNING GOAL: Development of musical memory and speed of response, most important elements in learning to play an instrument.

STAFF JOURNEY

Staff Game for a Small Room

EQUIPMENT: An oilcloth painted to represent the Grand Staff or a foam-rubber mattress cover with its cloth-backing side painted with the Grand Staff; a piano with narrow Staff Chart I behind the keys; a large Staff Chart II on the wall or screen, facing the children who stand in a row below the bottom line of the playing field. In addition, any other complete music staves, such as those that employ magnets or a moving note, may be used. Between the wall staff and the piano, as nearly side by side as possible, is placed a succession of Staff Charts II. Chairs, easels, etc., can be pressed into service for this purpose.

GAME: The children line up beneath the bottom line on the playing field. The first child runs to the bottom line, then to the wall staff, points to the same line and names it. Then he runs to each of the other charts, points to the same place, names it, and finally gets to the piano where he is aided by the chart behind the keys to play on the piano the tone that corresponds to the place he occupied. He returns to the line on the playing field, and that finishes his turn for the present, until all the children in the line have had a chance to run up and go through the same procedure on each successively higher space or line.

Only one child may be on the staff at a time.

LEARNING GOAL: There is considerable memory training here, as each child must retain the memory of the line or space from staff to staff as he completes his journey. Each child must also remember the name and place of the player before him so that he can take his place on the step above. Since only one child is allowed on the staff at a time, the staff is cleared between players and each child is forced to remember the line or space just occupied. As each child strikes his tone, all sing the alphabet name to the corresponding pitch, so there is constant association of sound with the staff position.

This activity was developed at the Third Street Music School Settlement, where the writer taught several classes in a small room.

STEPS

FORMATION: All players stand on bottom line G. IT stands on the G line in the treble.

GAME: IT turns his back on the other players, closes his eyes, and sings the C major scale descending—C-BAG-FED-C-BAG-FED-C. A rhythm suggested by this grouping of letters is recommended. (The two groups that are spelled "Bag" and "Fed" help to fix these letters from the descending musical alphabet firmly in mind.)

While he is singing, the others take their steps; the first step is on the bottom line G and then on each line and space above that. These steps must be carefully taken and counted silently.

Anyone moving when IT turns around must step back to the starting point. Before doing so, however, he may challenge IT by asking, "How many steps did I take?"

If IT answers correctly—remembering to count the starting place as "Step Number One"—the player must return to his former position on bottom line G. Otherwise, he may remain on the line or space he had reached.

The first player to pass IT while his head is still turned away, wins. The leader or teacher should play the corresponding sounds for all steps.

LEARNING GOAL: Foundation for understanding intervals. Ear training, staff familiarity, etc.

STORY TELLING
Rhythms and Pitch

EQUIPMENT: Cutout notes to fit on the staff, smaller cutout notes to fit on a smaller staff drawn on a piece of cardboard that can be passed around.

FORMATION: Players sit on the playing field. Depending on the number of children, the leader will suggest that they sit on the lines and spaces in an oval formation. If there are only a few children, only the treble part of the staff need be used. The size of the staff and the number of players will determine the arrangement.

GAME: Each child is to tell his share of a story that will be made up as the game goes along. Everyone starts swinging from the waist up in the same direction, first to the left. At first, each one may use only four syllables; this can be four separate words or less. Four cutout notes are arranged to make a measure on one line or space of the staff. For example, we might begin with a quarter, two eighths, and a half note.

As the player begins, he puts his hand down on the first note as he says the first word, and swings to the left; then as he says the next two words, he swings to the right, touching each eighth with two fingers held closely together (the index and middle finger). For the last word, he puts his hand flat down on the half note, and holds it there for two swings, while he prolongs that last word to two counts or two swings of his upper body. (See p. 196.)

The story might be, "John went to school." Pat the quarter for the "John," tap the two eighths with the fingers lightly for the words, "went to." For "school," pat the half note and keep dwelling on the word. Without losing its position, the hand allows itself to respond to the swing of the body with a slight sympathetic swing.

These words are chanted to the pitch of the line or space on which the notes rest, and this must match the location of the player on the staff.

He passes the cardboard staff with the notes to the next player who shifts them up to his line or space and continues the story in the same way.

After the cutout notes are arranged on the new staff location and have had appropriate words chanted to them, it is a simple matter for any child to play this rhythm on any tone at the piano or any other available instrument.

LEARNING GOAL: Concentration and coordination development. Preparation for lyric writing. Association of words to rhythm and association of pitch to line or space of the staff. Manual coordination specifically built up toward future instrumental study. Complete understanding of rhythmic patterns.

TAKE A GIANT STEP

FORMATION: One player becomes the Giant and stands above the top line of the staff. He faces away from the players while telling them what kind of step and how many to take. However, as soon as he has answered the question "May I?" that each player must ask before taking any step at all, Giant may turn around abruptly to check on the player.

GAME: All the players stand on bottom line G.

THERE IS ONE IMPORTANT RULE TO REMEMBER:

THE FIRST STEP IS TAKEN ON THE VERY LINE OR SPACE ON WHICH THE PLAYER IS ALREADY STANDING.

This forms the whole basis for reckoning intervals. For example: if instructed to take one baby step, the player who is stationed on bottom line G at the beginning of the game, will take a tiny, mincing step on that line and will end ON THAT SAME LINE. If told to take three baby steps, he will take a small step on beginning line G, then on the space above that, A, and finally the second line B.

At all times, the player must ask for the Giant's permission by saying, "May I?" If he begins the move before saying this, or if he takes the wrong kind or wrong number of steps, he forfeits his turn.

Variation I

With some groups it is possible to use two other kinds of steps: a "giant-3" step, and a "giant-5" step. For all giant steps, the player must lift his leg as high off the ground as possible, as in a goose-step march, about two feet off the ground. Failure to lift the foot this high when instructed to take a giant step results in a loss of turn.

The "giant-5" step is from a line to the second line above it, as from G to D. Or from a space to the second space above, as from A to E. In other words, begin on a space, skip the space above, and land on the space above the one skipped.

The "giant-3" step is from a line to the next higher line above it or from a space to the next higher space.

Variation II

With a younger group who do not have the patience to develop the "giant-5" steps, instruct the Giant that he may ask for a giant step but not more than one in a single turn. If Giant turns around before the step is completed, the player must finish the step; then, counting where he landed as his first step, he must step back and downward by baby steps to where he was when he started his giant step. This prepares the child for thinking intervals down as well as up.

As the children learn the game procedures, they should try to sing the letter names and pitch of each step, the leader helping as usual by playing the tones for each step on the piano or any available instrument.

At the beginning, it may be advisable to chalk in capital letters the name of each line, preferably several times—GGGGG, then BBBBB, etc. at the side as a continuation of each line on the staff and one small letter for each space. Remember that when stepping backward the players must remain facing forward as always.

The Giant may ask a player to take a certain number of steps backward as well as forward, but only one kind in one turn, not mixing backward and forward steps. Anyone arriving at the F line in the bass is entitled to take one giant step free. It is up to the

FIG. 94. The boy is illustrating a "giant-5" step, the girl a "giant-3" step.

Giant to prevent this, so he, as well as the players, must stay alert to the intervals.

Beyond the G line in the treble, he may not ask for any more backward steps.

This game is complex but well worth the effort in mastering it, as it is a complete introduction to the concept of intervals and how to name them by counting the alphabet letters including the start as Step Number One. This is difficult for beginning music students to grasp, so a game that can convey this technique is invaluable. Players should begin with the game of Steps before tackling this one.

LEARNING GOAL: Familiarity with intervals; finding out how they are reckoned and named.

TIME-VALUE HAND MOVEMENTS

The body should swing from left to right from waist up, and become coordinated with all the hand movements.

Quarter notes are slapped gently or patted with the hand directly on the cutout or written notes. There must be one swing to each pat for the quarter note.

Half notes are patted, with the hand going down and touching the note on the first swing which is to the left. The hand remains down with a slight sympathetic swing along with the body as it swings to the right. This is to create a slightly different muscular sensation that emphasizes the difference between the striking of the tone and the mere continuation of it. (See Fig. 68.)

EVERY CONTINUATION OR SUSTAINING OF A TONE ALREADY STRUCK WILL BE REPRESENTED BY A SLIGHT SYMPATHETIC SWING OF THE HAND WHICH REMAINS ON THE NOTE. In other words, the hand remains in the same position for the full duration of the sounding of the note. There is muscular discrimination between the hitting or articulation of the tone on its first beat and the added holding of that same note for additional beats.

Dotted half notes receive a pat on the first swing, and the hand remains in position for the remaining two swings, with the same slight swinging reflected in the hand which is held on the note for those two last sustaining beats.

Whole notes receive a pat on the first swing and the hand remains on the note for the remaining three swings with a slight swinging felt for each of those last three sustaining beats.

It requires great rhythmic poise and balance to sustain tones for additional beats. When two notes on the same line or space (but not necessarily of the same time-value) are connected by a tie (a curved line between the two notes), the hand strikes the first note *only* and remains down for the number of swings represented by the *combined* time-value of *both* notes.

All rest symbols are to be interpreted by raising both hands up in the air. The hands remain up in the air for the full duration of the swings indicated by the time-value of the rest symbol. (See p. 186.)

Advanced Time-Value Hand Movements

Four sixteenth notes receive a pat each from index, middle, ring, and little finger in successive order. (See Fig. 95A.)

Since one eighth note is worth two sixteenths and two eighth notes worth four sixteenths, the same fingers will pat the two

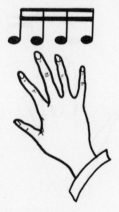

FIG. 95A.

197

eighth notes. The first eighth note is worth two sixteenths so the index and middle fingers held close together as a unit pat the first eighth and the last two fingers held close together pat the last eighth note. (Fig. 95B.)

FIG. 95B.

On this basis we can now interpret an eighth and two sixteenths: two fingers (index and middle) come down on the eighth, and the remaining sixteenths receive a pat each from ring and little finger consecutively. (Fig. 95C.)

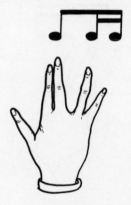

FIG. 95C.

If the two sixteenths precede the eighth, each of the sixteenths receives a pat from the index and the middle finger, one after the other, since each finger is worth only one sixteenth; then the eighth note which alone is worth two sixteenths receives a pat from the last two fingers held as one unit. (Fig. 95D.)

FIG. 95D.

In the typical Scotch rhythm of one sixteenth followed by an eighth and then another sixteenth, the first sixteenth receives a pat from the index finger; the eighth (Fig. 95E) worth twice

FIG. 95E.

as much, receives a pat from middle and ring finger held close together; the remaining sixteenth gets a pat from little finger.

The Dotted Eighth

Since a dot contributes an additional half to the value of the note it follows, a dotted eighth is worth three sixteenths and receives a pat from the index, middle, *and* ring fingers held together. The sixteenth note that would follow this dotted eighth note gets a pat from the smallest finger. (A separate sensation should be experienced in each of these three fingers that act as one.) (Fig. 95F.)

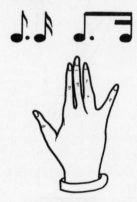

FIG. 95F.

As a special coordination exercise, skip around the room, synchronizing the eighth note tap (with three fingers) to the step and the sixteenth note tap (with the one littlest finger) to the short hop. A card on which these notes appear may be held in one hand. The tapping is done by the other hand directly on these notes.

The Dotted Quarter followed by an Eighth

This is one of the most difficult rhythmic coordinations to develop. Most teachers of beginning music students have ex-

200

perienced trouble in conveying this concept. Even when the concept is understood, the poise and balance demanded for its instrumental execution are often lacking. By maintaining the even swing of the body *against* the hand coordinations involved, using verbal stimulants that explain the rhythmic structure, mastery can be achieved more rapidly. It is simple to come down with the hand as one starts a swing, but to start a new swing in another direction and still leave the hand where it is and then to come down with the hand again before that second swing is completed is extremely complex.

FIG. 96. A coordination study for a dotted quarter note followed by an eighth note.

The quarter note receives a pat while the body swings to the left. The hand remains on the note while the body swings to the right for the dot, with a slight feeling of pressure from the index and middle fingers which ordinarily take care of the first of a pair of eighth notes. The dot is really the first of a *pair* of eighths but it is not sounded separately—it is only a continuation in sound of the quarter note. The remaining eighth is the second of the understood *pair* of eighths, but this is struck independently. Therefore before the second swing is completed,

201

the last two fingers (ring and smallest) come down on the last eighth note with one pat.

Once the swing is developed, coordinate with it these words: "Quarter" for the left swing and "press-pat" for the right swing. Change this to "Quarter" for the left swing and "Dot-eighth" for the right swing. The left swing represents the first count or beat which falls on the quarter, and the right swing represents the second beat which covers the sound-continuation indicated by the dot plus the separately struck eighth.

LEARNING GOAL: Development of rhythmic coordination with special emphasis on manual response.

TWO'S COMPANY

Eighth Note Version for Large Group

FORMATION: Pairs of children stand close together, facing the top of the staff, on each staff-line or space to be used in the game. They are scattered around the staff in the general formation of a ring around the empty center of the playing field.

GAME: One child is chosen to be the Runner and another the Chaser; they must always run on the outside of the staff circle.

Whenever the Runner makes a "safety-stop" beside any pair

FIG. 97.

of Eighth Notes and can name their location correctly, the Eighth Note who is standing farthest away from the Runner becomes the new Runner. He in turn is chased by the Chaser on the outside of the circle until he is caught and trades places, or until he makes a stop on a line or space occupied by another pair of Eighth Notes. If he can name their location correctly, he remains next to the Eighth Note closest to him while the one farthest from him becomes the new Runner.

LEARNING GOAL: Speed in naming the lines and spaces through the impetus provided by the chase.

"YOU NAME IT" TAG

FORMATION: Circle formation on lines of the staff; or children can be stationed on spaces only. (On a very large outdoor playing field where there might be more than a foot between lines, both lines and spaces may be used, but children should not be too close to each other.)

GAME: A Runner and a Chaser are chosen. They stand outside the circle, on opposite sides of the staff. Runner may stop once on Middle C during the chase. Otherwise he may save himself from being tagged only by getting on a line or space that he can name. However, it must be one occupied by a child in the circle.

If Runner can identify his safety stop correctly, he trades places with its occupant, who now becomes the new Runner.

Any Runner who fails to identify his safety stop correctly is made a Chaser. The former Chaser calls out, "I'll take —'s place!" (He may name any player occupying a line or space.) The player so named gives up his place and becomes the new Runner.

LEARNING GOAL: Speed in naming the lines and spaces through the impetus of the chase.

203

"YOU NAME IT" TAG and "TWO'S COMPANY" TAG
(For younger players)

Variation

Younger children who have not yet learned the names of the lines and spaces can call out the number of the line. The players in the circle will be stationed only on lines. Bottom line G is first line bass and the E in the treble is first line in the treble. The others are numbered accordingly. Since the players probably know the second line in the treble as the G line and the fourth line in the bass as the F line, they can name these as well as Middle C.

Learning these few points of reference and the number relationships of the other lines will deepen the child's understanding of the space relationships of the staff which are at the root of all music reading.

LEARNING GOAL: Preparation for staff reading.

WALK UP AND SMILE

GAME: Clasping hands, leader and group walk up the staff together, naming each line and space except A, where they nod and smile at each other instead. Then they walk down the staff the same way, saying the names of each line and space, remembering to nod and smile at A. In the treble clef, the group will sing the names on pitch.

On the next trip up the staff the children and leader say or sing all the names except A's and B's. Each time they walk up and down the staff they substitute a smile and nod for a new silent letter.

LEARNING GOAL: Increased concentration through the need for a carefully timed withholding of a response during a progression of similar responses.

WATCH OUT, HE'S COMING!

Preparation

Choose one child to be Middle C and another to be Leader of the Notes. Middle C stands on a black line or stick or strip under his feet. He keeps his eyes closed.

Leader of the Notes may write each child's initials on a line or space on a large music staff printed or drawn on paper, and show each child the position to which he is assigned; or the Leader may distribute pieces of music paper which show each child a certain note on the staff that will be his place. Another method is to have each Note-child wear a note card. A small piece of masking tape with the child's name on it may be attached to his staff location on the playing field.

GAME: The Leader of Notes taps certain Notes on the shoulder and urges them to move toward Middle C. He should select some from each clef so that when they approach as near as they dare, they surround Middle C.

As soon as Middle C claps his hands, Leader calls out "Watch out, he's coming!" Notes try to get back to the safety of their assigned places before Middle C can catch them. Middle C may not move until after Leader has called the warning, but then it is the survival of the fleetest. The first player caught trades places with Middle C.

The lucky Notes who are safe make up a little tune composed of their places on the staff, and play "themselves" on the piano.

LEARNING GOAL: Memory training through the incentives provided by the excitement of the game. Ability to relate playing field staff to small staff on paper. Instrumental application and creative effort toward combining a few tones into a tune or *motif*.

WHO HAS THE NOTE? I

EQUIPMENT: A small note, cut out of rubber or a black button with a short stem attached with tape. Make stem out of half a short paper match stick or anything else suitable and small enough so that entire note is not larger than a large button.

GAME: Players stand away from the staff. They hold their arms out, palm touching palm as in "Button, Button, Who's Got the Button?" Leader stands in front of the line of players. He holds the tiny note between his own palms and says, "I have a note called B (which belongs to the third line, G clef). Whoever gets the note must try to run to that line on the staff and then return the note to me before anyone else finds out who has it." The leader of the group had best be the first Leader in the game so she may make the instructions clear.

Leader puts his palms pressed together between the lightly closed palms of the players in the line. Even if he has dropped the note into the hands of the first or second player, he continues to pretend that he still has it.

When the player who really has the note thinks the attention of the group is absorbed elsewhere, in watching the Leader most likely, he makes a dash for the third line B in the treble, steps on the line, and runs back to return the note to the Leader. Anyone who tags him before he is able to reach the goal line, (in this case, B in treble) becomes the new Leader.

LEARNING GOAL: Concentration on a certain line or space of the staff.

WHO HAS THE NOTE? II

Variation for room with piano

FORMATION: Children stand on the different lines and spaces of the staff, close to each other. (Those on spaces can stand a little back of the players occupying the lines.) If necessary, they can stand on the staff in two such rows. Give everyone sufficient time to study his location. All players hold their palms lightly pressed together as in Who Has the Note? I, played out-of-doors.

GAME: Leader now goes from player to player holding the tiny note between his palms. He puts his closed palms between the closed palms of each player.

Waiting for a favorable moment, the one who received the note runs to the piano and plays his note, using as his guide the staff chart placed behind the keys, and the strips of black cardboard inserted in the keyboard at the keys which correspond to the lines of the staff. If he can do this successfully, he becomes the new Leader. If he fails, Leader continues the game.

If the children have progressed to the point where they know the keyboard well, the tagging feature in the outdoor version may be worked in. Whenever someone has received the note and runs to the keyboard to play it, he may be tagged by anyone in the line. If the tagger is successful in catching the note holder before he plays his note, the tagger must play his own note and that of the player whom he has caught. He then becomes the new Leader.

Instead of allowing any player to tag the note holder, the Leader may provide a variation by stating at the start of the game that only an upper or lower neighbor (one who stands on an *adjacent* line or space immediately next to him on either side) can tag him. If an upper or lower neighbor tags the note holder, he plays the note holder's tone first, then his own, and returns to the first tone, three tones in all. This makes it easier to hear the relationship of a note to its upper or lower neighbor.

LEARNING GOAL: Quick response, association of staff location and keyboard. Remembering note of player caught. Upper and lower neighbor concept.

ZIGZAG BEANBAG IN G MAJOR

EQUIPMENT: Beanbag and cutout sharp symbols.

FORMATION: One row of players on the spaces, one row on the lines of the playing field, facing each other.

Preparation

Place a cutout sharp to the right of each clef on the staff, at F, fourth line bass and F, top line treble. These cutout sharps for the signature are not shown in Figs. 98–101; instead, a sharp symbol appears before each F.

The row on the spaces stands nearest the clefs and begins on fourth space G (above the F line in the bass), and continues to first space treble which is no longer just F but now F sharp, as the sharp symbol in the signature puts us into G major and turns all the F's into F sharps. The player on F sharp wears a cutout symbol of a sharp over his arm or wears a paper-bag cap or note hat with a large sharp drawn on it.

The other row facing the space row begins on top line A of the bass clef and continues on Middle C, E, and G.

FIG. 98.

GAME: G in the bass, lowest note in the space row, throws the bag to A, the first player in the row of lines. As he throws, he sings his own name on pitch aided by the leader at the piano indoors or a specially prepared Autoharp out-of-doors. (See Musical Instrument for Out-of-doors, p. 51. For any game or activity in G major, the pegs of the F strings should be tuned a half step higher than the tuning used for C major, which has no sharps or flats.)

A throws the beanbag back to B, the second player in the space row. B throws it back across to C, second player in the line row, and so the game continues until it reaches the first space in the treble, the top player in the space row. This child must sing not only his first name but his last name too—F Sharp.

If F Sharp misses or forgets to sing, "F Sharp!" he must sing the whole scale as he hops on one foot a total of seven hops from the fourth space G in the bass all the way up to F sharp. Then he must bow low to the G immediately above his own F sharp station. This G gives the scale its key name—G major.*

After some experience with the arrangement of notes described above, transfer the same routine to an arrangement of notes an octave higher. Start on the G that is an octave higher than the G space with which we began in the previous arrangement. This high range will require voices that can sing the G above the top line of the treble. (Fig. 99.)

First row will begin with second treble line G and continue upward on lines B, D, and top line F sharp. The other row facing

FIG. 99.

it will be a space row, beginning on second space A, which is the note above the first note of our G major scale. The F Sharp in the line row must wear the F sharp symbol or cap and must always remember to sing his whole name. The top space in the row of notes on spaces will be G, the space directly above the top line. This is the first note we have used above the staff.

* See "Background for More Advanced Games," p. 41.

The throwing and singing is carried out exactly as before. It should be done all the way down the two rows as well as up.

FIG. 100.

There are many possible variations. A formation extending through two octaves may be tried after the arrangement of four notes in each row is mastered. (Figs. 100, 101.)

FIG. 101.*

After the game has been played a number of times in the suggested formations, it can be transferred to the keyboard. Each child repeats on the piano the sounds and names he has associated with the scale in the Zigzag Beanbag game.

LEARNING GOAL: Discrimination between notes on lines and notes on spaces. Understanding of alphabetical progression both up and down a scale as well as progression "step-wise" from line to space to line to space, etc. Introduction to structure of the major scale in terms of staff locations and alphabet names. Learning how to find the name of the key if you know the name of the last sharp. (In G major, F sharp is the first as well as the last sharp since it is the only one in the signature.) Ear training through singing each note as the beanbag is thrown successively higher or lower each time.

* Notes in Figs. 98–101 represent players, one row on spaces, another on lines, all in G major. (Signature is not shown.)

3. ADVANCED GAMES

ADD-A-NOTE I

EQUIPMENT: One large inflated ball, white soccer-type of ball with black lines painted on each end, or a beanbag that looks like a note.

NUMBER OF CHILDREN: Twelve or more, but fewer children can also play.

GAME: The children take their places in a diagonal row up the staff, on adjacent lines and spaces. The top child (on the highest

FIG. 102.

note) preferably on A, second space in the treble, has the ball and sings his note "A" on the pitch sounded by the leader. He passes the ball to the Note below him who sings out "G" on pitch. G passes the ball back to the starter A. A begins all over again, singing his tone as before and passing the ball down to G. G sings his tone and letter and passes the ball down to one more player, F. F sings his name and throws the ball to the starter.

Each time the ball goes back to starter, the routine is repeated, and each time the ball is handed down to one more player than the time before. If an error is made, the last "inning" is repeated. An "inning" consists of passing the ball from starter to the last player on that particular turn.

Naming Intervals

If going up the scale, the first player to start the ball is called First; the player next to him who reecives the ball is Second. As Second passes the ball back to First, the interval is called a Second. The other players are also called by an ordinal number: Third, Fourth, etc. As Fourth throws the ball back to starter (First) the interval or "throw of the ball" is called a Fourth. (See Fig. 102.)

When the ball starts at the highest note and is passed lower each time, the players are numbered so that starter is still First. The Note below him is Second, and so on down the line. The intervals are named the same way. From Third to starter is a Third.

This game lends itself to a number of variations:

Variation I

The ball may be bounced on the space or line on which the note-child is standing, then passed to one more player below; who also bounces the ball in his turn as he sings his name. Continue with the same routine of passing the ball back to starter before going down the line again, adding another player each time.

Variation II

Same as above except that player standing on first line in either staff will bounce his ball only once, player on the second line will bounce twice on that line, player on third line three times, etc.

This allows more time to dwell on the pitch, name, and staff location for each note.

Variation III

Start on any note, go up the scale instead of down, or both. Introduce other scales, etc.

LEARNING GOAL: Singing descending scale passages by name, (a difficult feat for most beginners); exercising the musical memory by the discipline of remembering how far up or down the ball has gone each time; introduction of interval jumps as the ball goes from the last child in the turn to the starter.

ADD-A-NOTE II

GAME: Players must try to sing every staff move throughout. First player runs to first (bottom) line G then runs to piano and plays only that G, using Staff Chart I as a guide. Second player steps on G and space above (A); then returns to start, G. He finishes by playing G, A, and back to G—three tones—at the piano. Third player steps on G, A, B, leaps back to start, and plays these four tones on the piano.

The *jump-back* is important as it acts out the difference between "steps" to neighboring notes (as from line to space to line), and the "jump" or interval from a note to another note which is *not* neighboring.

Each player begins at bottom line G, steps on the succeeding

213

lines and spaces, adding one more than the preceding player. From the last note, he jumps back to the first line. Each player finishes by playing on the piano the steps and the jump back to starting point.

Fourth player steps on G, A, B, and C, then jumps back to start, G. The jump is named after the player. In this case, since he is Fourth, his jump is a Fourth.

Proceed as far as space E in bass, then begin again, using space C (second space in bass) as start. C becomes First and plays only his C.

Go only an octave higher, then use Middle C as new start. Start is again First and plays only one note. All these moves have been in C major, no sharps or flats.

Variation I

Introduce a new signature, one sharp, then two and three; play the game in the new key. Place a cutout sharp on the notes under the domination of the signature. Place sharps for signature on staff chart also.

Variation II

Upon reaching the last step up in the step-wise progression of a single "inning," jump back to start, then back and forth between the highest and lowest notes. This allows more time to assimilate the interval, going both up and down. Singing it several times helps to strengthen the impression.

ADD-A-NOTE III

EQUIPMENT: White piano-key costumes and beanbag note.

FORMATION: Same as in "C Major White Keys" p. 178.

GAME: White Key C passes the beanbag note to White Key D after C sings his alphabet name on its pitch. Each player who has the note in his hand at any time sings his name on pitch. D passes the note back to C. C passes to D who in turn adds a note by passing to the next player E. E hands the note back to C; they pass it back and forth twice as they sing their names and listen to the interval (in this case, a major third).

The routine continues, the last person to get the note in each "inning" handing it back to the starter, who lets him repeat this act so everyone can hear the new interval. This can also begin with the high C as starter. A new note is added each time because it is passed down to one more player than before. There is always the same repetition of the passing of the note from the last player on that "inning" to the starter.

Variation I

After finishing the game on the playing field, each Piano Key plays "himself" in a keyboard version of the same game.

Variation II—(Introduction of other keys)

EQUIPMENT: Black-key costumes, note hats, cutout sharps and flats in addition to white-key costumes and beanbag.

GAME: Lay the sharps or flats down on the staff to form a new key signature. Arrange the players as before. Piano Keys affected by the signature will wear the black-key costume and note hats showing the required sharp or flat. They pass the note and sing in the Add-a-Note III routine, progressing to a keyboard version of the same game.

LEARNING GOAL: Acquaintance with the intervals in C major and other new keys through reading, keyboard experience, singing, and multiple sensory-motor responses.

CHORDS WITH A SMILE

FORMATION: Three children go up to the staff. The first group stands on the first, second, and third lines of the bass clef. Each says or sings his note, and together they listen to the chord they form. A simple chord, called a triad, is composed of three tones, each a third apart (in C major, every other white key played simultaneously).

The children should stand in a straight vertical line; those on the second and third lines stand behind the child on the first line. Another group comes up and stands on the first, second, and third spaces, in a straight line, the two higher Notes directly behind the lowest one. All sing or say their names.

The next group comes to the second, third, and fourth lines, saying their names. Each successive group of three takes its place in the same manner, occupying successively higher positions. Once the placement is mastered, the same trick is used as in Walk Up and Smile, p. 204.

GAME: Any A is required to smile instead of singing her name or she may whisper it. It will be interesting to discover how many times the A will occur in different chords. Try another letter on another round of the game.

LEARNING GOAL: The concept that one tone may be a component part of several different chords. An invaluable preparation for the future study of harmonization.

CHROMATIC COUSINS

EQUIPMENT: Eight white-key costumes and five black-key costumes.

NUMBER OF CHILDREN: Thirteen (or more).

GAME: The Piano Keys arrange themselves in keyboard pattern, as in Black Key Scramble, p. 176.

All the Black Keys show their sharp side. The lowest C turns to the Black Key standing behind him and also between himself and White Key D. He embraces or shakes hands, saying, "I'm your cousin C."

Try to sing this to the pitch of Middle C.

The other one, the Black Key, answers, singing on the pitch

of C sharp, "I'm C Sharp. Let's have a talk, Cousin." One sings C, the other C sharp; they repeat this back and forth several times. Then they hold hands and dance around the small area where they were standing, each singing his tone, one after the other.

Now White Key D turns to the Black Key behind him (and between himself and White Key E). The dancing and song-conversation proceed as before, with D singing his tone and D Sharp answering with his, several times.

Then E says, "I have no cousin here now, but he'll be here on the way down," or words to that effect.

F picks up the conversation with his Black Key cousin, F Sharp; they are followed by the same routine between G and G Sharp, then A and A Sharp.

B weeps and says, "I don't have a Black Key sharp cousin, but my other Black Key cousin will be here on the way down." The top C says, "I'll go see my brother Middle C" (or sister). "I'll be right back and we'll start the trip down." He runs to Middle C, they shake hands and sing C-C-C-C, alternating the lower C with the higher. He returns to his place at the top of the White Keys.

The Black Keys turn their costumes around so that the flat-cutout is in front.

We now begin the trip down to visit the Black Key "flat-cousin." C on top weeps, "I have no Black Key flat-cousin. B, go visit yours."

B turns to the Black Key between himself and White Key A, introducing himself to his Black Key flat-cousin, "I'm B. Are you my cousin, B flat?"

"Yes, I'm your cousin, B flat." They sing, "B, B flat."

This happens all the way down the chromatic scale.

F has no Black Key "flat-cousin," and tells E to visit his.

The game is like a little play script, and can be improvised upon.

The idea that each cousin is just a half step away should be worked into the dialogue. If a piano is available, take all the players to the keyboard. Play the chromatic scale up and down, singing sharps for the black keys when going up and flats for the black keys going down. Play at the back edge of each key so that all the black and white keys in the chromatic scale are easily seen side by side in a regular succession.

C, C sharp, D, D sharp, E, F, F sharp, G, G sharp, A, A sharp, B, C (note where two whites come together). C, B, B flat, A, A flat, etc.

LEARNING GOAL: Familiarity with the chromatic scale. Recognition of half steps through ear training, keyboard experience, staff reading, and dramatization as in the exchange of greetings between a White Key and its sharp or flat Black Key "cousin." (White Key should take a half step up to meet its sharp or a half step down to meet its flat). The achievement of learning all the half steps is so vital to further music study that this could almost be considered the peak of the entire course of games.

DAMPERS

Preparation:

Observe the action of the dampers inside a grand piano when the music rack is removed and the lid is propped up. Play a chromatic scale from Middle C up, at the back edge of the keys near the wooden panel, singing the name of each note:

For the ascending chromatic scale, sing: C, C sharp, D, D sharp , E, F, F sharp, G, G sharp, A, A sharp, B, C.

For the descending scale: C, B, B flat, A, A flat, G, G flat, F, E, E flat, D, D flat, C.

(Review Chromatic Cousins, Half Steps and Whole Steps pp. 38–40, 216.)

Count all keys from C to C and notice the arrangement of

218

the raised dampers. Each is next to the other which means that each tone is a half step apart. As you will remember from "Background for More Advanced Games," p. 38, notes that are a half step apart (in tone-vibrations) are represented on the piano by dampers which are next to each other.

Now play the C major scale, composed of all white keys from Middle C to the next higher C, and hold all the keys down. Compare the two scales in number of notes played, etc. Observe the design formed by the raised dampers. Play more major scales and observe that the design formed by the raised dampers is the same. Each child gets a chance to recreate it, starting from any note on the piano.

GAME: Thirteen children, who will pretend to be the Dampers sitting on the strings inside the piano, sit down on the floor. Several of the remaining children officiate at the piano, playing the chromatic scale from Middle C up to the next C. Depending on the order in which the Dampers have settled themselves, each one will sing one note of the scale, rising and singing his name when he hears that tone played on the piano. Each child, when he has finished singing his tone, will sit down again as the real damper resumes its place.

New players come to the piano to play the chromatic scale going down. As a group member plays top C, the last seated child rises, sings C, and sits down again as the tone is not held indefinitely. Then B is played, and the next to the last child rises, sings B, sits down again. The playing and the rising, singing, and sitting of the Dampers continue throughout the entire descending chromatic scale.

Major Scale Arrangement of Dampers

The playing team now begins on Middle C and plays all the white keys up to the next C. This is the C major scale. Instead of singing the alphabet names, leader or another member of the group sings do-re-mi, etc. pulling up a corresponding

Damper. She skips one wherever there is a whole step in the scale.

After some practice the members of the group must be able to respond to the do-re-mi of the major scale, and the right Dampers must rise to the occasion. If they fail to do so, and are left sitting, they pay a forfeit.

If the playing team will hold down all the keys in the scale there will be two pairs of children standing close together—the third and fourth in the row and also the seventh and eighth. The others are separated by sitting Dampers.

Remember to skip a child for the whole step! The ones whose notes are not played must remain sitting on their imaginary strings. Each one must sing his do-re-mi name as he rises to sing the sound of his piano key. Anyone who rises when he should not, gets a point against his score. Change the children around so that everyone is forced to think all the time.

LEARNING GOAL: Chromatic scale and structure of major scale.

FAMILY REUNION

Script

ANNOUNCER: Let's look in on the members of the C Major Scale as they hold one of their famous family reunions at the Grand Staff Palace.

FIRST MEMBER: I'm Daddy, the head of this family. People call me Tonic. I'm very restful. Every discussion ends with me.

SECOND MEMBER: I'm D, the second member of the C major family. I sit a whole step away from Daddy Tonic.

THIRD MEMBER: I'm E, the third member of the C Major Scale and I sit one whole step away from the second member of the family.

FOURTH MEMBER: I'm the fourth member of the family. F is my name. I'm Grandmother. When Mother's busy I run the house for her. I always sit in a rocker close to the third member of the family, so close that I'm just a half step away. I'm called Subdominant.

FIFTH MEMBER: I'm Mother and next to Daddy I'm the most important. Most of the time I feel I am the most important member of the family and certainly the most active. People say I'm very bossy and that "Action" is my middle name. My real name is Dominant and I really dominate. Nothing stands still when I'm bustling about. You'll always find me one whole step away from Grandmother Subdominant.

The sixth member explains that he always stands a whole step away from Mother Dominant.

Seventh member stands one whole step from Sixth, and he says, "They call me Leading Tone, because I'm the oldest brother and I am very active like Mother Dominant. But I like to go to Daddy with everything. You can't keep me away from Daddy Tonic. I stand close to him always."

The eighth member of the family adds, "Do you wonder who I am? I'll tell you a secret. I'm Daddy's twin brother. We're so much alike no one can tell us apart so I'm called Daddy Tonic too."

Daddy Tonic calls, "Meeting's over!" Everyone leaves his place. Then he calls the meeting to order again. The trick is for everyone to find his place again and to be able to describe his position, duties, and characteristics as in the dialogue above. The dialogue suggested by the director may be freely elaborated upon by each member of the scale at its family reunion. First time through is a rehearsal. Second time, the real show is "on the air."

At first, the alphabet names of the scale are omitted. After considerable experience with this scale material and excursions into various scales, the alphabet names may be introduced into the script. Cutout sharps and flats are worn by those affected by the signature.

The C major scale can be arranged easily on the playing field, but it is helpful at first to act out the other scales away from the staff and near the piano.

Variation

The scale members, wearing their piano-key costumes, take their places on the staff, spreading out diagonally in order to allow the distance of whole step or half step to be made clear.

They begin with the singing of the scale, each member contributing his tone, name, and family position. Then they build three chords: tonic, dominant, and subdominant.

Tonic takes Third Member and Dominant with him to the piano and together they play their respective sounds which form the tonic chord. They return to their places on the staff.

Subdominant steps out and takes Sixth Member and Daddy Tonic's twin brother to the piano. Together they play their respective sounds which form the subdominant chord. When they return to their staff locations, Mother Dominant takes Leading Tone and Second Member to play the dominant chord. Leading Tone and Second Member return to their places, but Mother Dominant remains and beckons to Daddy Tonic to bring Third Member back to the piano for the final statement of the tonic chord.

LEARNING GOAL: An introduction to the concept that within a key the chords built on the different degrees in the scale perform special functions. Understanding of the role of tonic and dominant. Study of new major scales.

THE KEY AND THE SHARP

EQUIPMENT: Cutout sharp symbols, large enough to wear as handcuffs. Large note symbols, quarters, half notes, dotted half notes, and whole notes. Black elastic cords to attach a quarter note. Note hats may be worn instead.

FORMATION: Children wearing notes form a circle near the edge of the staff or on the staff, depending on size of staff playing field. One child is chosen by a counting-out process to be the key (Key of G or Key of D) and another to be a Note, who wears a sharp when he is caught by the Key.

Counting-Out

The children say the musical alphabet twice, and the one who is F in the third round is the Note who must be caught and handcuffed ("sharped"). The letter next to him, G, becomes the Key of G. This parallels the actual musical situation where the name of the key is derived from the alphabet letter above the letter (or scale degree) that gets the last sharp. (This is for major keys with sharp signatures only.)*

GAME: The children form a circle on the staff or if the staff is small, around it. At the start, Key of G is outside the circle and F within. Since F is allowed to run only on a space or line bearing the name F, he may run in and out of the circle to get from one F on the staff to another.

KEY OF G: I'm the Key of G.

KEY OF F: I'm the Half Note (or whatever denomination he is) on F.

KEY OF G: I'll catch you.

KEY OF F: You can't.

Key of G chases F in and out of the circle. The circle Notes try to help F by letting him through their lines whenever he wants to go out, and closing ranks quickly against the pursuing Key of G. The circle may move around so there will be a constant supply of new defenders of the F lines and space.

When G finally catches F, he "sharps" (handcuffs) his cap-

* See p. 42.

tive and leads him off to prison in the signature, as the group sings to the tune of "He's a Jolly Good Fellow":

> Let's put him into the signature,
> Let's put him into the signature,
> Let's put him into the signature,
> And he will never get out.

Each of the clefs is considered a guard for his prison. The space to the right of each clef is reserved for the signature, which must appear in duplicate in both the bass and treble.

After the first round of the Key and the Sharp is played and F is safely imprisoned in either the bass (F) or treble (G) prison, the group must count-out for another F who will be caught and clapped into the empty prison. All captured Notes must stay in prison for the remainder of the game.

For most groups this much of the game would be sufficient. If anyone wishes to continue further, choose a C and the D after him to be the Key of D. C goes into the center of the circle and runs on all the C's. The Key of D tries to catch C. The F Sharp in the signature may help Key of D, but he must remain in his signature. When one C is captured and put into the treble signature, the game is played again with the new Key and another C. This C when captured goes into the bass signature.

LEARNING GOAL: Getting to know all the F's on the staff and all the C's. Introduction to key signature. Acquaintance with Key of G and its F sharp, and with Key of D and its signature of two sharps, F sharp and G sharp. Realization that the name of the key is both the letter and degree of the scale above the last sharp in the signature.

MAJOR SECONDS, MINOR SECONDS

Preparation

Place index and middle finger on white keys C and D. Slide them back, feeling for the black key. These two keys that do have a black key between them are called a major second (*second* because the interval is from a *first* to a *second* alphabet letter and *major* because the two keys are a whole step apart).

When the same two fingers slide back on white keys E and F, they have no black key to feel.

These two tones, E and F, a half step apart, are called minor seconds. Find other major seconds and minor seconds starting on a black key.

GAME: Divide children into two teams. Each one wears a card showing one note from the chromatic scale. One player goes to the other team and looks for a partner with whom to play a Major Second.

He may choose a Note either a whole step above or a whole step below. The two players then go to the piano and play the Major Second. The last player goes to the other team and looks for a Minor Second partner, who goes up to the piano with him while they play the Minor Second. The last player up always goes to the opposite team and looks for a Major Second if the last one played was a Minor; and a Minor Second if the last one played was a Major. If he cannot find one, or takes too long, another player from his group comes up and resumes the choosing of partners. Minor Second partners walk to the piano, close together; Major Seconds, further apart.

Other matching of partners can be devised.

LEARNING GOAL: Review of half steps and whole steps as a preparation for the understanding of any scale.

PASS THE SHARP

EQUIPMENT: Cutout sharps.

GAME: The players sit on the lines and spaces of the staff. To begin, use G major for the key in which the game will be played. Its signature, one sharp, is placed on F, both treble and bass.

225

Another sharp is passed up and down the line of sitting children. Every time it comes into the hands of any F on the staff, that F must quickly rise before passing the sharp on to the next player. If the teacher can play the corresponding notes for each child as he receives the sharp, valuable key-consciousness may be developed. Any F failing to rise must pay a forfeit.

Variation

Each child takes the name of the line or space on which he is sitting. The F's are pointed out particularly in a preliminary "warm-up." These must not be allowed to receive the sharp as it is passed up the staff from hand to hand.

The F's try to make their neighbors forget this by extending their hands to receive the sharp. Anyone guilty of giving the sharp to an F who already *is* a sharp according to the signature must sing the G major scale up and down with letter names, hopping on the corresponding lines and spaces.

Sometimes the sharped F forgets himself, and then he too must pay a penalty. He is not permitted to touch a sharp.

When the players become more experienced, the game goes into the key of D with a signature of two sharps, F $\sharp$ and C$\sharp$. In this game, both F$\sharp$ and C$\sharp$ must be prevented from getting the sharp that is being passed around.

LEARNING GOAL: Concentration on a key signature. Singing letter-names of notes in G major songs.

SHARPS, FLATS, AND NATURALS

Rise and Shine

EQUIPMENT: A cutout sharp.

GAME: All the children squat on the lines and spaces diagonally up the staff. A cutout sharp is passed from child to child. As each child receives the sharp he stands up to show that it raises him up a half step. Anyone who fails to raise himself may be required to leave the game. The last one left on the staff wins.

FIG. 103.   Sharp, flat, natural.

Go Down Flat

EQUIPMENT: A cutout flat.

FORMATION: Children stand on lines and spaces diagonally up the staff. As soon as the flat comes into a child's hands, he squats down. Anyone failing to do so has a point against him.

Natural Winner

EQUIPMENT: Cutout sharp, flat, and natural.

GAME: Pass both sharp and flat symbols along the line of children, one from each direction. Any child who receives both at one time becomes a Natural, earns a point, and wears the Natural symbol. Four points earn a whole note; first one to gain a whole note, wins.

LEARNING GOAL: Acting out the required reaction to a sharp or flat symbol.

STAFF ON YOUR HANDS

Bass Staff

Hold left hand in front of you, palm up. Think of the smallest finger as the lowest line of the bass staff (G), the ring finger as the second line (B), the middle finger as the middle or third line (D), the index finger as the F or fourth line, and the thumb as the top line (A). LISTEN AS THE SOUNDS OF THESE LINES ARE

227

PLAYED, AND WIGGLE THE FINGER THAT CORRESPONDS TO EACH
SOUND.

Now go to the piano and, turning the hand back to its natural
position, play the five staff-lines of the bass staff, using for each
line the finger that represents it. Play G with the fifth or smallest finger, B with the ring finger, D with the middle finger, F
with the index finger, and A with the thumb. Avoid numbering
the fingers; think only of the lines of the staff.

Return to your place and hold the left hand as before, palm
up. Someone will play the different lines on the piano and you
are to respond by wiggling the corresponding finger.

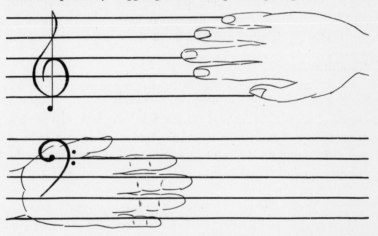

FIG. 104. The fingers of the left hand, palm up, represent the
lines of the bass staff; those of the right hand, palm down, the lines
of the treble staff.

Treble Staff

Hold the right hand in front of you, palm *down*, fingernails
showing. Thumb will stand for bottom line E, index finger
for second line G, middle finger for B, ring finger for D, littlest
finger for top line F. Wiggle the corresponding finger as the
sounds of these lines are played. Then go to the piano and

play these staff-lines with these specially designated fingers. Now that you have felt each sound for each finger, return as before and as someone else plays the sounds for you, wiggle the corresponding finger.

Spaces

So far we have dealt with the staff-lines only. Using only one staff at a time, follow a song written on the blackboard or in a songbook by sticking the index finger of the opposite hand into the space between the fingers to indicate the spaces, and touch the correct finger when a line is used for a note. For instance, if a note appears on the first space in the treble, poke the left index finger between the first and third staff-lines represented by the thumb and index finger of the right hand. Wherever a note appears on a line, simply touch that particular finger that stands for that line.

To follow a piece that uses both clefs, wiggle a "finger-line" for a note on a line and make a scissors-like movement with the two "lines" that form the boundaries of a space whenever a space is used. For Middle C and the spaces on either side of it, move the right hand close to the left for B, a little higher for Middle C, and still higher for D. In other words, the right thumb seems to mark the location of these notes in the space between the hands which at all other times are held about two inches apart from each other. Learning a new song by following the lines and spaces on the hands is an excellent way to make oneself concentrate on the written melody.

LEARNING GOAL: Integrating a manual response into the co-ordinations required for reading.

STRIP STAFF "FOLLOW THE LEADER"

EQUIPMENT: Ten strips of dark colored cardboard one-quarter inch wide and about nine inches long, one white strip also one-quarter inch wide and nine inches long to be used for Middle C. This strip has a short black line drawn in its center. Ten additional white pieces tapered from a quarter-inch wide at one end to allow it to be slipped under the wooden panel at the back edge of the piano key to about three-quarters of an inch in width for the last three inches. This distinguishes these pieces as spaces and provides the necessary contrast to the line pieces. Each strip is to be inserted at its corresponding key, as in the Strip Staff, p. 27. (See also Fig. 21B, p. 24.)

GAME: The children form a line outside the staff near the clefs. The first in line crosses the staff from the clef side on bottom line G. He may choose to walk, hop, slide, dance across it. One child recently crossed his arms and pranced across like a Cossack. Anything that is not unreasonable or violent adds to the fun, for the next three children who will come across on space A, line B, and space C must "follow the leader" who was the first player. Each player crossing the staff ends by going to the left of the keyboard, where he chooses either a black strip for a line or a white one for a space, inserts it at the key corresponding to the line or space he traversed, plays it, and sings its name. He may play a rhythm on that key, and each of the players who follow his example in style of locomotion must also imitate his rhythm on the piano key corresponding to the point where he crossed the staff.

The fifth player, coming across on third bass line D becomes a new leader and makes the journey across in his own way. One player who sat down and started to slide across, met with rebellion from his followers, so it is wise to make it clear that originality is welcome but must stay within bounds. The next three players cross the staff on their successive lines and spaces following D's example.

The rest of the game continues in the same way. D also inaugurates a new rhythm as he plays his line. A will be a new leader, then E, followed by B. Each leader is followed by three players. The player who must cross on top treble line F may choose whichever style he wishes. If there are not enough players for each to take a separate line or space, the available players continue taking turns until the staff is completed.

Ascending Variation

PREPARATION: Review Banners Flying, one step to each swing of both arms for quarter notes; one step on the first of two swings (starting with a backward swing) for a half note; one step on the first of three swings for a dotted half; one on the first of four swings (beginning with a backward swing) for a whole.

After these are mastered, two running steps to one backward swing will represent two eighth notes on a downbeat (either the first or third beat in 4/4 time) and two running steps on a forward swing of both arms will represent two eighth notes on an upbeat such as the second or fourth beats in 4/4 time. In 3/4 time, the downbeat, which is the first of three beats (an *odd* number), comes on a backward swing every *other* measure, so two running steps could represent two eighth notes on a swing in either direction.

FORMATION: The players draw lots for their particular line or space. These consist of slips of music paper, both staves present with one note indicated on a line or space in either clef. The players form a line at the edge of the clefs according to the note they have drawn, bottom line G going first as usual.

GAME: As each player comes through the staff on his line or space he acts out the time-value for as many measures in 4/4 time as the length of the line demands. If two measures would be required to get across, both measures could be alike, or one measure could be all quarters and the next could be two half notes. With more experience, various time-values could be mixed in each measure. The rhythmic pattern acted out on the playing field is then played on the corresponding piano key after the strip has been inserted.

As in the previous game, the first of each four players could create the rhythmic design and the next three would have to follow it. Thus every fifth player (G, D, A, E, B, and F for example) would be pace setters. Since F is the top line and last player to cross the staff, the game should start again, but this time G, A, and B at the bottom of the staff would follow the measures as they were arranged by F, so the next leaders in the second round would be C (second bass space), G (fourth bass space), D above Middle C, A (second treble space), and E (top treble space).

Descending Variation

After reaching F at the top for the first time, the players could come across their lines and spaces again, except in this variation they would be coming down the staff. Coming down the staff, the new leaders would be F, B, E, A, D, and G, if we proceed as we started, changing rhythms with every fifth player.

Another Variation

We could make a rule that when any player blunders, the next player may become a new leader rhythmically. Also, the lots drawn could have, instead of one note drawn on the Grand Staff, a rhythmic pattern for two measures. The notes would all be on the same line or space. The possibilities for variation in this activity are limitless, so new elements may be woven in, each time the game is tried. Other intervals can be designated as signals for a new leader; for instance, try every fourth player, or every sixth player, etc.

LEARNING GOAL: This game encompasses many aspects of music-learning: concentration on the staff-lines and spaces, their relation to the keyboard, listening carefully to the rhythms and imitating them, and awareness of the intervals a fifth apart: G, D, A, E, B, F, C. These are of utmost importance in later music study.

FIG. 105.

APPENDIX

GAMES FOR SMALL INDOOR AREA

ELEMENTARY

All Set for School
Alphabet Soup
At the Market
Banners Flying
Beanbag Games
   Bag in the Basket
   Staff Board Game
   Where Was I?
   Zigzag Note (C Major)
Big Note Cutout
Blindman's Buff
   High or Low
   Swinging Stick
Candy Carols
Cheer Leaders 3/4 and 4/4
Conducting Designs
   Butterflies and Bows
   Conducting Two Christmas
      Carols

My Name Is Susie
Counting on the Fingers
Counting Measures I and II
Crossing the Road
Feeling the Beat
Fists and Fingers
Follow the Leader I and II
Forfeits
Game of Silence
Gameboard (played with movable notes)
Grab Bag
Harmonica Pete
Hopovers
Hot or Cold
Keeping Score I and II
Measure Rulers
Nicknames
Note Hockey

INTERMEDIATE

C Major White Keys
Silent Rests
Staff Journey

Story Telling
Time-Value Hand Movements
Zigzag Beanbag (G Major)

ADVANCED

Add-a-Note I, II, and III
Family Reunion
Major Seconds, Minor Seconds
Pass the Sharp

Sharps, Flats, and Naturals
Staff on Your Hands
Strip Staff "Follow the Leader"

GAMES FOR OUTDOORS OR LARGE INDOOR AREA
(Gymnasiums)

ELEMENTARY

Acquaintance with the Staff
As We Have Done Before
At the Bridge
B–C–D, Run from Me
Bait the B–C–D
Banners Flying
Bar-Lines and Staff-Lines
Beanbag games
   Center Base
   Dodge Note
   Leader and Group
   Target Note
Black and White Coin Toss
Blackberry Hill
Blindman's Buff
   High or Low
   Note Exchange
   Swinging Stick
Change Bases
Chasing Time-Values I and II
Conducting—

Cover the Spaces
Drop the Note
G-G-G, Come Get Me!
G-Man
G-G, Pull Away!
Gameboard
Heavy, Heavy Hangs Over
Hidden Notes
Hide and Seek
Hopovers
Hunting He Will Go
Let Me In
Line and Space Tag
Magic Carpets
Middle C, Can't Touch Me
Moving Notes
Musical Chairs
Note Hockey
Notes and Piano Players
Pass It to Me I and II
Pass the Sharp

Player and Note

Prisoner's "Bass"

Pussy in the Corner

Red Light, Green Light

Relays

Run Around I and II

Space Chase I and II

"You Name It"

INTERMEDIATE AND ADVANCED

Add-a-Note I, II, and III

Black Key Scramble

Call Ball

Chords with a Smile

Chromatic Cousins

Cross Tag (Upper Neighbor)

Dampers

Eighths and Quarters

I Send

The Key and the Sharp

Running from the Rests

Sharp (Musical Spud)

Steps

Take a Giant Step

Two's Company

Walk Up and Smile

Watch Out, He's Coming!

Who Has the Note?

"You Name It" Tag

Zigzag Note in G Major

GAMES FOR RHYTHM, TIME-VALUES, AND COORDINATION

ELEMENTARY

Among Friends

At the Bridge

At the Market

Banners Flying

Big Note Cutout

Blindman's Buff

   Swinging Stick

Chasing Time-Values I and II

Cheer Leaders 3/4 and 4/4

Conducting Designs

   Butterflies and Bows

   My Name Is Susie

   Two Christmas Carols

Counting Measures I and II

Counting on Your Fingers

Dotted Half Note Chase

Dreaming Clef

Farmer in the Dell

Feeling the Beat

Fists and Fingers

Grab Bag

Hunting He Will Go

Keeping Score II

Let Me In

Measure Rulers

Nicknames

Notes in the Measure 3/4

   and 4/4

Pat on the Back

Post Office

INTERMEDIATE

Eighths and Quarters
Running from the Rests
Silent Rests

Story Telling
Time-Value Hand Movements

ADVANCED

Strip Staff "Follow the Leader"

KEYBOARD GAMES

Add-a-Note II and III
Bag in the Basket
Black Key Scramble
Chasing Time-Values I
Chromatic Cousins
C Major White Keys
Dampers
Drop the Note
Family Reunion
Game of Silence
Hidden Notes
Hot or Cold
Major Seconds, Minor Seconds

Moving Notes
Musical Chairs
Nicknames
Notes and Piano Players
Post Office
Staff Journey
Staff on Your Hands
Story Telling
Strip Staff
Watch Out, He's Coming!
Who Has the Note II
Zigzag Note in G Major

MUSIC FOR THE CONDUCTING GAMES

Music for use with Conducting Designs, Counting Measures, and Counting on the Fingers should be made up exclusively of the five primary time-value units emphasized in this book—quarter, half, dotted half, whole, and eighth notes. Since the main objective is to give the child immediate success in feeling first the beat and then the whole measure as a unit, the music should be as free as possible of syncopation, dotted rhythms, and upbeats.

It is not easy to find music that meets such restricting specifications. If a song meets all the requirements except for one small infraction, it can still be utilized; often the irregularity can be

238

changed without material damage to the song. An occasional dotted rhythm, syncopation, or upbeat can be accepted if most of the song is in the five primary time-value units necessary for our objective.

For example, two old songs, "Sweet Betsy of Pike" and "Old Hundredth" (also known as the "Doxology"), both have upbeats, but the melody is a continuous flow of quarter notes. Nothing could make the child feel the beat more strongly than a succession of quarter notes, each note receiving one beat. The upbeat can be taken care of by making a wide sweeping gesture with the right arm such as one makes in asking an audience to rise to its feet. The conducting will begin on the "one" of the first *complete* measure.

The Time-Value Parade music on p. 79 can be advantageously used for these elementary conducting and beat-feeling games. By presenting a succession of identical time-value units, they prepare the beginner to recognize these primary time-value units as they occur in the musical literature.

Although the conducting games are based on 4/4 and 3/4 time signatures, music in 2/4 and 6/8 may occasionally be used.

In 2/4 time, use a "down, up" motion for each measure or combine two measures (two quarter notes in each measure) into one measure of four quarter notes, and use the usual 4/4 conducting design.

When using a song in 6/8, mentally change each measure of six eighth notes into two measures, each containing three quarter notes, and use the 3/4 triangular conducting pattern for each of these imaginary measures.

If the lyrics do not seem suitable for certain groups, omit the words and hum the music, since it is the music that is needed.

Above all, play or sing all pieces at a moderate tempo as the beginner needs ample time to grasp the measure as a unit and to make the necessary physical responses.

For 3/4 conducting designs, use the Andante from *Orfeo* by Gluck, the "Minuet in G" from *The Anna Magdalena Book* by Johann Sebastian Bach, the main themes from such famous waltzes as the "Blue Danube," the "Emperor Waltz," and "Tales from the Vienna Woods," all by Johann Strauss, the "Merry Widow Waltz"

239

by Lehar, the "Skater's Waltz" by Waldteufel, "Valse Triste" by Sibelius, and the "Waltz Song" from Gounod's opera, *Romeo and Juliet*. The well known song, "Poor Wandering One" from the Gilbert and Sullivan opera *Pirates of Penzance* and the famous Largo from Handel's opera *Xerxes* could also serve admirably.

For the 4/4 conducting designs, use "Ase's Death" and "In the Hall of the Mountain King" from the *Peer Gynt* suite by Grieg, "Chanson Triste" by Tchaikovsky, "Country Gardens," by Grainger, "Evening Prayer" from Humperdinck's opera *Hansel and Gretel*, and the Largo from Dvořák's *New World Symphony*.

All of these can be obtained at any large music library or major music store.

Many favorite songs which can be found in popular collections for group singing meet our requirements. In 3/4 time, there is the well known "After the Ball Is Over," "The Band Played On," "Bicycle Built for Two," "East Side, West Side," and "Jeanette Isabella." In 4/4 time, use "Angels We Have Heard on High," "Au Clair de la Lune," "Gaily the Troubadour," "Go Down Moses," "Jacob's Ladder," "Long, Long Ago," "Love's Old, Sweet Song," "Volga Boat Song," and "Wondrous Love."

Innumerable songs for our purpose can be found in the many volumes of the graded school songbook series such as *The American Singer* (American Book Co.), *Music for Living* and *New Music Horizons* (Silver Burdett), *A Singing School* (C. C. Birchard) and *Together We Sing* (Follett Publishers).

For the five-and-six-year-old group, many suitable songs can be found in *The Complete Nursery Book* by Inez Bertail (Lothrop, Lee and Shepard), *Music Time* by Evelyn Hunt (Viking Press), *The Singing Time* by Satis Coleman (John Day), *Songs to Grow On* by Beatrice Landeck (E. B. Marks and Co.), and *Songs Children Like*, compiled by the Association for Childhood Education International.

"Deaf Woman's Courtship," "Going to Boston," "Go Tell Aunt Rhodie," "Hey Betty Martin," "Paw Paw Patch," are among the best for our purpose in *Songs To Grow On*, by Beatrice Landeck.

In *The Complete Nursery Book*, by Inez Bertail, the following favorites also serve as excellent material for the beat-feeling and measure-feeling activities:

"Baa, Baa Black Sheep"
"Cobbler, Cobbler Mend My Shoe"
"Dance, Thumbkin, Dance"
"Ding, Dong, Bell"
"Hot Cross Buns"
"Johnny Had a Little Dog"
"Little Sally Waters"

"Old King Cole"
"Old MacDonald Had a Farm"
"Soldier, Soldier, Will You Marry Me?"
"Taffy Was a Welshman"
"Ten Little Indians"
"Twinkle, Twinkle, Little Star"

"Cuckoo, Cuckoo Calls from the Wood"
"Lavender's Blue"

"Oranges and Lemons"
"Lazy Mary"*
"Pussy Cat, Pussy Cat"*

Try the following from *Songs Children Like* (Association for Childhood Education International):

"Chinese Lullaby"
"Christmas Candles"
"The Ducks" (Indonesian song)
"Jasmine Flower" (Chinese folk song)

"The Lazy Man and the Busy Man" (by E. Hunt)
"Louisiana Lullaby"
"Springtime has Come" (Japanese)

"Good Morning to All"
"Heissa Kathreinle"

"Morning Is Come"
"Wind Song"

The eight-to-twelve-year-olds will find a wealth of material in *Sing Together*, published by the Girl Scouts of the United States of America:

* These songs are in 6/8 time in this collection, so mentally divide each 6/8 measure into two 3/4 measures and sing slowly.

"Allelujah"
"Au Clair de la Lune"
"Coo-coo"*
"Dakota Hymn"
"Flowers Are Dying"*
"Foxlease Vesper"
"Girl Scouts Together"
"Gone Is Autumn"*
"Great Tom Is Cast"*

"Louisiana Lullaby"
"Ode to Joy"
"Old Hungarian Round"*
"Old King Cole"
"Rainy Day Round"*
"The Tinker"*
"When That I was a Tiny Little
    Boy" (Shakespeare)
"White Sand and Grey Sand"*

IN 3/4 TIME

"Basque Lullaby"
"Good Night"*
"Hark to the Chimes"
"Let's Have a Peal"

"Lovely Evening"
"Morning Is Come"
"Slumber, Slumber"

The music recommended here for the beat-and-measure-feeling games will provide only a nucleus for your musical library. Its sole purpose is to serve as a guide for the selection of additional material.

* Each of the songs starred is a round.

INDEX

Musical Chairs, 150
Music Educators Journal, xiii
"My Country 'Tis of Thee," 36
"My Name is Susie," 103

Natural, 42; game, 227
Neighbors, Upper and Lower, 74, 180, 206
Nicknames, 151–154
Notation, 3–15, 183, 196–201
Note cards, 48, 71, 132, 179, 200
Note Exchange, 91
Note hats, 48
Note Hockey, 154
Note Pickup, 137
Notes and Musicians, 155
Notes in the Measure, 156–157

Octave, definition, 40; recognition, 73, 128, 142, 164, 169, 177, 183, 189, 209, 214, 217
Oilcloth, 46, 93, 190
On the Double, 77–79
Orientation, 13–53, 25
Outdoor games, 236–237; musical instrument for, 49–52

Parade of the Time-Value Regiments, 74–79
Pass It to Me, 159
Pass the Sharp, 225
Pat on the Back, 160
Phrase, eight-measure-, 98, 100; four-measure-, 34, 148, 152, 158
Piaget, xix
Pianissimo, 130, 140
Pipe-cleaners, 27, 28, 47, 102, 109, 111, 137
Pitch, xiii, 34; associated with staff, 50–52, 60, 89–90, 163, 169, 192, 194; comparison of, 81
Play Schools Association, 53
Playing Field, 44–46
Plywood notes, 46
Post Office, 162
Prisoner's "Bass," 163
Psychology of childhood, xix–xx
"Pussy Cat, Pussy Cat," 157
Pussy in the Corner, 164

Quarter note, 12
Quiet activity, Big Note Cutout, 86; Candy Carols, 93; Conducting Designs, 102, 109; Counting on the Fingers, 113; Feeling the Beat, 122; Fists and Fingers, 125; Game of Silence, 130; Grab Bag, 131; making a model keyboard, 19; making staff charts, 20–29; sharps, flats, and naturals, 226; Silent Rests, 185; Story Telling, 191; Time-Value Hand Movements, 196

Reading readiness, 114–116
Records, xxi, 240
Red Light, Green Light, 165
Relating staff to self, 59, 166
Relays, 168–169
Rests, 183; interpretation 185, 197
Rhythm, xiii; arm-swinging as beats, 12–15, 63–66, 74–79; articulation, 78, 181, 196; balance, 79, 122, 196, 201 (*see* Beats); body-swinging, 122, 161, 181, 192, 196–202; conducting games, 96–113 (*see* Co-ordination); manual response, 181, 192, 196 (*see* Measure, also Phrase); poise, 123; prolongation of syllables, 12, 64, 87, 92, 154, 192; step and swing, 74–79; syllabification, 15 (*see* Time-values); verbalizing, 12–15, 34, 87, 181, 182, 192, 202
Rhythm and Pitch, 191
Rise and Shine, 226
Run Around, 169
Running from the Rests, 183

Scale, 39–43 (*see* Major)
Scoring system, 84, 143–144, 154
Seconds, Major and Minor, 224
Sensory-motor responses, 215
Sharp, 42–43, 185, 222, 225, 226
Sharps, flats, naturals, 226
Signature, key, 31, 164, 224; time, 31–34, 239
Silence, 130, 185
Silent Rests, 185